83,000
Square Miles
no lines, no waiting…

Printed in the United States of America by
Mennonite Press, Inc., Newton, KS.

ISBN 1-880652-94-3

Library of Congress Catalog Card Number: 98-60963

Cover design by Bill Bolte
Book design by John Hiebert
Photography by Steve Harper

83,000
Square Miles
no lines, no waiting...

Kansas Day Trips by Steve Harper

A publication of The Wichita Eagle and Beacon Publishing Co.

This book is dedicated to my wife Charlotte, and my daughters Alicia, Rachel and Audrey. And to the pioneers who were smart enough to know a great place when they found it, and the native and naturalized Kansans who have helped Kansas maintain its status as a friendly and prosperous state.

Thanks for the help

Many offered information, guidance along the way

I would like to thank the county historians, librarians and postmasters and the hundreds of other friendly folks I have met and talked with during my ongoing travels throughout Kansas. Without their generous help and obvious love of Kansas history I would not have been able to compile much of this information.

I would be remiss if I didn't mention the late Forrest Hintz, my good friend and mentor of the back roads and byways. Forrest taught me many things about people and reporting. And he knew that Kansans are, by their nature, a friendly lot and that if you greet people with a smile and a handshake they will always welcome you into their lives. He was right.

Forrest was a columnist for The Wichita Eagle-Beacon. Over a period of 20 years he wrote informative, delightful stories about Kansas and Kansans. One of his series of stories, "The Vanishing Towns of Kansas," was a popular Monday feature in the newspaper. Through his insightful writing, he reaffirmed for readers that good, old-fashioned values are alive and well in Kansas. He retired from The Eagle in 1983 and died in 1984. His words, however, will live on forever.

There are several authors of source documents whom I would like to thank. Through a great deal of effort Virginia Lefferd, a member of the Kansas Trails Council, was able to compile a much-needed list of hiking, bik-ing, horseback riding and canoeing trails in Kansas. Her booklet, "An Index to the Trails in Kansas," provided the trails information in this book. An updated trails book will be published in 1999 by the University Press of Kansas.

I also obtained invaluable historical information from two books written by John Rydjord, dean emeritus of the Graduate School, Wichita State University — "Kansas Place-Names" and "Indian Place-Names." His penchant for detail and love of history shine brightly through his writing. If you find a copy of either book, buy it and enjoy.

"Natural Kansas," a book by Joe Collins, vertebrate zoologist with the Museum of Natural History at the University of Kansas, was very helpful as I traveled around the state. Through his accurate descriptions, line drawings and pho-tographs I was able to identify a number of plants, species and ecosystems.

I would like to thank Brian Logan, cartography manager for the Kansas Department of Transportation, Bureau of Planning. Logan was responsible for reinstituting the 1970s-style Kansas Transportation Map. The map indicates all of the physiographic provinces in Kansas, so map users will know when they pass from one geological feature to another. The geological information was provided by the Kansas Geological Survey.

The folks at the Kansas Museum of History and the Kansas Historical Archives in Topeka were also helpful in providing information.

A special thanks goes to Sara Quinn for her delightful cover illustration and inside drawings on the original edition of the book. And I, slow of hand, am eternally grateful to Glenda Elliott for her accurate typing skills, good cheer and positive feedback about the project.

For all those who love history, a word of thanks to Kevin Bailey, the his-tory teacher who backstopped me on the many historical references. Also many thanks to the thousands of Kansans who submitted the more than 500 trivia questions used in the Kansas Trivia Game published in The Wichita Eagle in 1985.

And what about the editors, the pick-ers of nits?

Many thanks to Chuck Potter, my good friend, and editing mentor on the original Day Trip book. Chuck is also a masterful pool player who, as my team-mate, repeatedly showed several senior editors the meaning of 8-ball humility. We never lost. Chuck talked me through agonizing changes in copy and made the book easier to read.

And special thanks to Tom Suchan, my old (and I mean that in the kindest way) newsroom boss who gave real meaning to the term "patience of Job." Prior to the original book being pub-lished, Tom put up with my missed deadlines and helped me soften the edges of my sometimes pointed com-mentary, thus making it a kinder, gen-tler book.

I would also like to thank The Wichita Eagle's publisher Peter Pitz for responding to our readers' requests to reprint "83,000 Square Miles: No Lines, No Waiting," and Kate Christopherson in our marketing department for her hard work to bring it all together.

Happy trails!

Table of Contents

The rock formations in Mushroom State Park, located at the north end of Kanopolis State Park, have a strong appeal for youngsters who can't resist climbing or lounging on the unusual forms.

It's time to explore Kansas, a state with more surprises than most folks can imagine.

On the road again and still loving every minute of it.

Although I started my Kansas exploration odyssey more than 27 years ago, I know for certain there are still plenty of friendly folks to meet and thousands of miles of back roads, small towns and hidden wonders to explore.

The pleasure of travel can be even more rewarding when the windows are rolled down and the radio turned off. Only then can you fully experience nature's fragrances and sounds, or feel the warm air and the sun on your face. Anyone who has ever heard the melodic warble of western meadowlark on a cool summer morning knows exactly what I mean.

As I stated in the original Day Trip book, "Highways are good for getting us from one point to the next, but they're more functional than fun." That statement is as true today as it was in 1990. The roads that inspire us to explore are often the ones we breeze by on our way to somewhere else.

I know, I've done it. And if you're like most folks, you've probably passed up more than your share of opportunities to wander the back roads of Kansas. That's the point of this book — to return to yesterday, to follow a whim and make that turn to an unknown destination, to leave the fast lane so you can slow down and find out what it really means to be a Kansan.

Kansas is a big and beautiful state with 105 counties and — depending on who you ask — 81,778 to more than 82,300 square miles. Just to be on the safe side I chose "83,000 Square Miles" as a title. Who knows, maybe we'll acquire more of Missouri if the Missouri River shifts a little to the east. Or perhaps Kansas will expand some during the heat of the summer. Hey, it's possible.

The only trouble with traveling in the 14th largest state is that there are no signs saying "Start Here." The intention of this book is to supply you with a good mix of starting points, destinations that will allow you to better know your home on the range, the 34th state. If you begin right now you might see a good many places by the end of the century, and in the process contribute in some small way to the economic stability of a small town cafe or grocery store.

All of our counties have unique features. No two reflect the same history, elements of mystery or occasional flights of fancy, but all are filled with good people. Because Wichita is Kansas' largest city I have chosen it as a common point of origin for the majority of our trips, but you can pick up the trail from wherever you live.

Some of these day trips will take considerably longer than others, but I guarantee you that all of them will be interesting and informative. But to make that happen you have to promise to take your time, to stop whenever and wherever the notion strikes. Heck, after these journeys your kids might even end up with a better knowledge of Kansas history and geology.

Although many of us have visited hundreds of places, there are always more to explore. It would take a pretty sizable book, one that wouldn't fit into your car, to cover all of the natural and man-made attractions of the Sunflower State.

Each of our trips will involve a little history, a little lore, some geology and the names of places and folks that will provide you with further guidance. Some of the businesses or post offices may have closed or changed since I first visited them, but the most fundamental rule of exploration remains unchanged: Ask someone else.

In one fashion or another we'll visit the four corners of Kansas, travel alongside dozens of meandering rivers and streams, and cruise back roads through small towns. Any experienced back-road traveler knows that detailed maps can be one of your best resources for nook-and-cranny exploration.

Perhaps the best and most portable guide to back road travel is DeLorme's Kansas Atlas and Gazetteer. The 80-page book has incredible detail, so good that you would have to actually work to get lost.

At your fingertips is every existing road, paved or unpaved. You'll know where roads end and where they pass through small towns that may or may not show up on a Kansas Transportation Map. In fact, many of the boom-bust towns that ceased to exist years ago are represented in DeLorme's book. You'll also be able to locate all city and county lakes as well as large watershed ponds. The maps also feature the name of each creek, no matter how small.

At the front of the Atlas is an index of place names, map features, federal reservoirs, state parks, natural features, historic sites, area attractions and walking tours, as well as fishing and hunting opportunities. The book also features wildlife viewing areas, river paddling entry points and hiking areas.

Other good sources of day trip information are local Chambers of Commerce and the post office in most small towns. Kansas Visitor Centers at Goodland, Olathe, Bonner Springs and Caldwell have loads of pamphlets from virtually every small town in Kansas, and they're free. Don't feel bad about taking one of each, that's what they're for, to entice you to visit whatever the brochure is promoting.

The Army Corps of Engineers and the Kansas Department of Wildlife and Parks offices at the big reservoirs also have detailed pamphlets and maps explaining facilities and costs. Each of the regional Wildlife and Parks has a boatload of pamphlets as does the headquarters in Pratt. Give the department a call at (316) 672-5911 and ask for a set of state fishing lake maps.

The secret of exploration is to stay loose. Clear your mind of work and the trials of daily life. Turn down any road that strikes your fancy and enjoy Kansas as it is — a wonderful state with a rich history, friendly folks, architecture that will sometimes astound you, abundant wildlife and a cornucopia of geological formations.

Expect to be surprised by the subtle and striking changes in topography. Pay no attention to time except to have a good one. Stop and talk to folks, visit museums, and always choose a cafe for lunch instead of a fast food place.

And don't forget your camera or camcorder. Take plenty of pictures or shoot videotape, preferably both. Kansas sunrises and sunsets are hard to beat, so imagine their beauty set behind the hundreds of scenes that you'll see while traveling. Early morning and late afternoon are optimal times for making great pictures, but don't pass up a shot just because the light isn't perfect.

The best thing is to pick a destination, then head out and explore. Stop at small-town grocery stores or historical museums and ask about local areas of interest. I haven't met an unfriendly person yet, and I've met a lot of folks in 27 years of cruising our highways and byways.

A land of colorful canyons and unusual vistas

Barber County gives you the feel of being in a John Ford Western

Imagine for a moment a scene where two rawhide-tough cowboys coax their stylish quarter horses toward the crest of a rust-colored butte. At the top they pause for a while, silhouetted against the orange, cloud-laced sky, the sun already halfway below the horizon. Within a half-hour the long red fingers of waning sunlight turn to twilight blue then meld into the crisp, black star-specked canopy of night. It's the end of another average day in the Gypsum Hills of Barber County, and you missed it.

But there is more to this unusual landscape than buttes and mesas and spectacular sunsets. There are gently rolling terraced wheat fields, often the first to be cut during the annual Kansas wheat harvest. The grain from those initial cuts is traditionally taken to Kiowa for testing and storage.

To begin your day trip to Barber County take K-42 southwest from Wichita to where K-2 splits off to Harper, then at Harper take U.S. 160 west to the little town of Sharon, the Hebrew word that means "plain." From there drive south on a county blacktop to Hazelton (named for town founder Rev. J.D. Hazelton), then take K-14 to Kiowa.

Kiowa, only a few miles from Oklahoma, is another one of Kansas' many small towns that appears to be doing well economically, and it looks good, too. On the north edge of the downtown sits a small but attractive city library. Next door is the Kiowa Historical Museum — (316) 825-4727 — housed in the old city hall and fire station. Through volunteer labor and gifts of family heirlooms from area families, the folks at the museum have put together an excellent display of Kiowa historical memorabilia. It's a fine museum that still houses one feature of the original interior — the jail in the back.

Kiowa also has the distinction of being the first place where Carry Nation — an imposing woman who stood 6'1" and dressed in black — chose to grind her ax against demon rum. The ax used by Nation, an unusual all-metal affair, is on display at the museum. On the south wall is a circuit

The rugged, cedar-dotted beauty of the Gypsum Hills is a surprise to many travelers who venture down U.S. 160 west of Medicine Lodge.

camera photograph (very wide-angle) of the 1929 Kiowa Rodeo, an event that was second only in size and fame to the Cheyenne Frontier Days Rodeo in Wyoming. The image shows rodeoers, including two women, and toward the left in the front row is Will Rogers, old "I-never-met-a-man-I-didn't-like" himself. And if you look closely you'll notice the same guy standing at both ends of the image. Ask the museum volunteers how that was accomplished. Museum hours are 2 to 5 p.m., Tuesday and Thursday.

In front of the First State Bank in downtown Kiowa is a petrified tree stump. Standing five feet tall and rock-solid, it has become a town icon of some historic note. But few citizens, save Clark McIlree, chairman of the board at the bank, know its origin. According to McIlree, around 1900 the tree was pulled from the Cimarron River bed west of Alva, Okla., then brought to Kiowa. It sat in front of a jeweler's shop for several years until it was moved a half block east, and placed in front of the bank. It's been there ever since.

Another interesting part of Kiowa's history involves its starting line role in the famous Cherokee Strip Run of 1893. It was one of the five Kansas border towns along the 57-mile starting line.

March 23, 1966, was a black day in Kiowa history. More than eight down-town businesses were destroyed or severely damaged during an early morning fire. Six of the eight businesses rebuilt within a year of the disaster, and a seventh, the theater, was rebuilt with community contributions. Kiowa deserves the title of a "town too tough to die."

West of Kiowa is Hardtner, and according to the greeting painted on the water tower it's the "Gateway to Kansas." With the exception of Main and Central, all Hardtner streets are named for Indian tribes. On the north end of Main is Achenbach Memorial Park. It's a fine little hillside park with good picnic and playground facilities. The park also has a restroom with a mountain scene painted on three sides, and it's pretty good painting.

The countryside around Hardtner is honeycombed with caves, each filled with several species of bats. In fact, of the more than 500 caves in Kansas, the majority are found under the Gypsum Hills. According to the Kansas Speleological Society, Comanche County leads the pack with 128 caves, and Barber County has 117. One Comanche County cave is reputed to have Indian pictographs.

Two-and-a-half miles west of Hardtner is the southern terminus of Gypsum Hills Drive. Take the road north to visit some of those buttes and mesas I was going on about at the beginning of this chapter. But drive slowly, and preferably at sunrise or sunset.

For the first 13 miles the road is relatively straight, the terrain evolving from flat farmland to the rich, red, cedar-dotted rolling hills, the trademarks of this beautiful landscape. At 13 miles you have the choice of turning left (west) for a back-road look at the hills or you can continue on the blacktop and pass through one of the most breathtaking parts of Barber County. The landscape is right out of a John Ford western, where sharply defined red hills rise to flat crests topped with tufts of prairie grass.

Cedars accent a landscape filled with colorful canyons and Panavision vistas, sprinkled with a wide variety of wildlife including white-tailed deer, mule deer, bobcat, tarantulas and Rio Grande turkeys. Anyone who visits this part of Barber County without a camera and plenty of color film is missing a grand opportunity to record some of Kansas' most unusual images.

Both drives, the back road and blacktop, will take you to U.S. 160. The only difference is that you end up in different places. Since you can see the blacktop part any time, I suggest you take the more leisurely back-road drive.

At the point where you need to make a decision about which road to take, you'll see "Flower Pot" mound off to your left. It's about two miles north-west of that intersection and is shaped like the dirt from a flowerpot when it's dumped upside down. Local history has it that several settlers were burned at the stake by Plains Indians on the Flower Pot mound.

You can drive to the mound by going west for about a mile, then north for another mile to just before where the road dead ends. It looks like a pri-vate drive, but isn't. You'll be on a road that passes through open range, so watch out for the cattle.

As you continue on, some 12 miles from where you started your back-road drive, the road should deliver you back to U.S. 160. If it doesn't then you're lost, but if you don't tell anybody, I won't mention it either.

If you do end up on U.S. 160, and I suspect you will, then I recommend you drive west for about six miles then take the road north to Sun City. Drive slow and breathe in the countryside. Keep your camera handy, the window rolled down and turn off that radio!

All this is prime wildlife country, so don't be a bit surprised if you see any number of the critters who make a living in the Gypsum Hills. Early or late in the day are the best times, but one time, just past midday, I saw a large bobcat with a cottontail dan-gling from its jaws, prancing down the railroad track. Once the bobcat

saw me he quickly disappeared into the prairie grasses.

Sun City has the look of an Old West town. The main street is dirt, and if you're there at the right time you'll see more cowboys than you can count. If you get there on any day but Sunday you'll find a place to have lunch and catch up on the local gossip. The post office, particularly early in the day, is a good place to meet folks and get infor-mation. Don't be shy — Kansans are a friendly lot and always willing to help a stranger.

One of the interesting things about Sun City is the fact that it is three towns in one, at least that's how it is known to the locals who know the town's mining history. The main sec-tion is Sun City, but a row of houses that runs south from the west edge of the main drag is called "Stringtown" and another area on the west side is called "Mexico." Ask the locals you meet to explain where the names originated. Only the old-timers will know.

The social center of Sun City is Hathaway's, a fine family tavern where Buster and Alma Hathaway served up their legendary 24-ounce frosty schooner of beer for 50 years. Sadly though, my good friends Buster and Alma have both passed away. But Hathaway's, under the ownership of Steve Hathaway, still serves ice-cold beer from the legendary 24-ounce

schooner. The folks there also serve burgers to round out your meal and offer a selection of soft drinks and chips if a burger and a beer don't suit your tastes.

Folks from all over Kansas continue to stop at Hathaway's during their Gypsum Hills tour. Maybe because it is one of the few remaining businesses where the customer has a choice of a two-holer or one-holer. It's an interest-ing experience for those who've never experienced the ambiance of an old-time outhouse.

But if you only stop in Sun City to take in the late afternoon light as it rakes across the downtown buildings, you won't be disappointed. No matter what your reason, Sun City is the place to be on a Saturday afternoon in Barber County.

There are two pleasant back road drives out of Sun City; however, both will take you out of Barber County. Just north of town the road parallels the Medicine River to the small town of Belvidere. South, on the road you came in, is a road that cuts off toward Wilmore. Both are very pleasant and worth the extra time.

From Sun City I recommend the road southeast to Lake City. Turn south at Lake City for a scenic five-mile drive back to U.S. 160. At the highway turn left (east) for more views of the Gypsum Hills on your way to Medicine Lodge.

The annual Gyp Hills Trail Ride draws horseback riders from across Kansas. The journey takes riders through a landscape that is largely unseen from the road.

There's a lot to see in Medicine Lodge and even more if you visit there on the last weekend of September. The Indian Summer Days Celebration features the Kansas Championship Ranch Rodeo. The rodeo highlights a weekend of activities in and around Medicine Lodge.

The rodeo showcases full-time wranglers from 10 of the largest working ranches in Kansas. They compete at penning cattle, wild cow milking, bronc riding, calf roping and other activities associated with day-to-day ranching chores. There's also an arts and crafts fair in town. Top all this with a parade on Saturday and you've got a pretty good reason to visit Barber County. The Kansas Muzzle Loaders Association adds an additional air of the Old West by having an encampment each year during the Indian Summer Days Celebration.

If you really want to see something big, then drop by for the next Medicine Lodge Peace Treaty Pageant in 2000. It's a three-day mega-event held every third year, and it involves just about everyone in Medicine Lodge who can walk and talk.

The pageant marks an important treaty drawn up between the Plains Indians and the U.S. government. Thousands of tribe members from the Arapaho, Comanche, Kiowa, Cheyenne and Apache tribes gathered a few miles

An icon of the Gypsum Hills, an old and weathered cowboy boot adorns a fence post south of Sun City.

Bathed in the late afternoon light, a jar of preserved peppers sits atop an old cash register at Hathaway's, a popular watering hole in Sun City.

west of the confluence of Elm Creek and Medicine River in October 1867 to strike a peace agreement in which the tribes agreed to relocate on reservations in Indian Territory (later known as Oklahoma Territory). The treaty, however, was never carried out.

Great orators such as Satanta, Ten Bears, Silver Brooch, Little River and Bull Bear delivered eloquent speeches about the importance of the land and a treaty that was to profoundly affect their lives. The United States was represented by Kansas Gov. Samuel J. Crawford, Indian Commission president N.G. Taylor, Indian agent J.H. Leavenworth and a sprinkling of brevet major generals. H.M. Stanley, the reporter who worked with David Livingston in Africa, was there, as was Harper's Weekly illustrator John Howland, along with Kit Carson and Jesse Chisholm.

What the pageant boils down to today is three days of family-oriented pageantry that is action-packed and unrivaled in citizen participation. Of the 2,300 or so residents of Medicine Lodge, 1,700 to 2,000 are directly involved.

If you can't visit Medicine Lodge in September then drop by another time and visit Carry Nation's home and the Stockade, a museum run by the Medicine Lodge Historical Society. The Nation house is open Wednesday through Sunday from 1 to 5 p.m., the Stockade Monday through Friday from 10 a.m. to 5 p.m. and Saturday and Sunday from noon to 5 p.m. Admission to each is adults $2, children $1, senior citizens $1.50.

On the east side of town on U.S. 160 is the city park with hookups, and a good picnic and playground area. If you're of a mind to, you can walk down to Elm Creek for an afternoon wade in the cool, clear waters of a Gypsum Hill stream. For more information, call the Medicine Lodge Chamber of Commerce at (316) 886-3417.

Other annual events in Barber County include the Spring Wildflower Tour on the second Saturday in May and the Gyp Hills Trail Ride on the second and third weekends in May. There is an annual Labor Day celebration in Kiowa, and the Barber County Fair is held in August each year at Hardtner.

Did You Know?

What was Derby originally named?
El Paso

How many speeches did Lincoln make in Kansas?
Four

What Kansas college boasts the only antique automobile restoration program in the country?
McPherson College

What does the ship stand for in the state seal?
Commerce

Name the six Kansas counties on Mountain Standard Time.
Cheyenne, Sherman, Wallace, Greeley, Kearny and Hamilton

What is the highest temperature ever recorded in Kansas?
121 at Fredonia and Alton in 1936

John H. "Doc" Holliday placed an advertisement for his practice in the Dodge City Times, June 8, 1878. What kind of doctor was he?
Dentist

What is the distinctive shape of the Mid-America All-Indian Center?
An arrowhead

What was Bat Masterson's career after he left Kansas?
A New York sportswriter

What three animals appear on the flag of Kansas?
Bison, horse, oxen

What was the prairie coal used by settlers in Kansas?
Bison chips

Because of the many Eastern European people who settled there, southeast Kansas was originally known as what?
The Balkans

Dance hall girl Alice Chambers, who died of natural causes, was the last person buried here.
Boot Hill

Jazz great Charlie "Yardbird" Parker was born in Kansas City, Kan., in 1920. What was his legal name?
Charles Christopher Parker, Jr.

What does the mighty Wurlitzer organ in Century II weigh?
34 tons

Who was the Kansan who was instrumental in getting basketball in the 1936 Olympic program?
Forrest C. "Phog" Allen

What town in Kansas can boast of having the first woman rural mail carrier in the United States?
Pleasanton in Linn County (Mary Reynolds Hazelbaker)

What is the smallest Kansas county by area?
Wyandotte

What is the only river in Kansas that flows north?
Nemaha River

The Marais des Cygnes River in eastern Kansas is French for what?
Marsh of the Swans

Who was the first woman elected to the U.S. Senate in her own right?
Nancy Landon Kassebaum

In what year did the honeybee become the official state insect?
1976

Wichita is an Indian word meaning what?
Scattered lodges

What town is known for its Czechoslovakian heritage?
Wilson in Ellsworth County

What is the name of the official governor's residence?
Cedar Crest

What is the largest county in the state?
Butler

What is the Halloween festival held in Independence called?
Neewollah

Who is considered the father of the Sante Fe Trail?
William Becknell

In what year was the Kansas state fair held in Peabody?
1885

In 1924, a new car appeared on the market. What Kansan was it named after?
Walter Percy Chrysler of Ellis in Ellis County

Amelia Earhart was aviation editor of what magazine?
Cosmopolitan

What Kansan was the first female treasurer of the United States?
Georgia Neese Clark Gray

The gentle giant of Cherokee County

There's no hiding Big Brutus in the southeast corner of the state

Under the definition of 'humongous' should be a photograph of Big Brutus. If you've heard of, but never seen this metallic juggernaut, it's probably because it's tucked away in the Mined Land Wildlife Area of Cherokee County, the southeastern cornerstone of Kansas.

But one thing is certain, you can't miss it when you get there. It's the "thing" that looms from the trees just south of West Mineral — the "thing" of nightmares and legends, for if Kansas is the "Land of Ahhhs," then Cherokee County must truly be the "Land of the Awesome."

To get there from Wichita take U.S. 54 east to just past Augusta where you pick up K-96 to Fredonia. From there take K-47 east to U.S. 59, then go south on U.S. 59 to U.S. 160. Continue east on U.S. 160 for about 17 miles until you see the sign directing you south on a county road to Big Brutus. If you go too far you'll end up in Missouri.

Once you get close to West Mineral you'll have no problem spotting it. It's the bright orange monster towering 160 feet over the otherwise flat, tree-studded landscape.

Brutus, owned by the Pittsburg and Midway Coal Company, is the only machine of its kind, and is the second-largest coal digger in the world; the largest is in Ohio. It was put together on-site, much like a giant erector set, near Hallowell. Construction began in June 1962 and was completed by May 1963.

It took 150 railroad cars of component parts and 52 men to complete the task.

During its 10 years of operation, the electric-powered Big Brutus ran 24 hours a day. It dug an 11-mile trench from Hallowell to West Mineral while scooping up approximately 7,500,000 tons of coal from 10,000 acres of land. In the end it was judged unprofitable to operate, backed out of its hole, turned off and left to rust.

Now ask yourself: Is that any way to treat a genuine Bucyrus-Erie model 1850-B? Of course not. Even a metallic beast has a heart, of sorts.

Fortunately, in the early 1980s Vic Boccia, a grocer from West Mineral, and LouNell Bath of Pittsburg decided — separately, but at the same time — to restore the big machine to a useful purpose, a second chance of sorts. Through their joint efforts they were able to talk P&M officials into deeding Big Brutus and 16.7 acres of land to Big Brutus Inc., a nonprofit organization.

"It's almost unbelievable," said an amazed Boccia in 1985. "They just gave it to us, and then paid $100,000 to have it painted and cleaned up."

Shining big, bright and orange in the summer sun, Big Brutus was dedicated on July 13, 1985. Now open to the public, it serves southeast Kansas as a mining museum, RV park, outdoor entertainment center and prime tourist attraction.

Visitors to Big Brutus in Cherokee County are dwarfed by the world's second largest land mover.

Hours are 10 a.m. to 4 p.m. Admission is $3 adults, $2.50 seniors, $2 for children 6-12, free to those 5 and under. For more information, call (316) 827-6177.

And as long as you're in the area you might want to hike, camp, canoe, fish, watch birds or hunt in the Mined Land Wildlife Area surrounding Big Brutus, more than 14,500 acres of public land that was once mined for coal. Mining began in Cherokee and Crawford Counties in the 1800s. Within the MLWA are 1,500 acres of public waters, and each of the 200 lakes has been managed to benefit certain fish species.

The strip pit lakes provide some of the finest largemouth bass, red-eared sunfish, warmouth, bluegill and channel cat fishing in Kansas, and pit #30 is a year-round trout fishery. Each of the 200 lakes have been managed to benefit certain fish species. To find your way around the MLWA maze you can pick up a map from the Wildlife and Parks office in Pittsburg, or call (316) 231-3173.

The view of one of the strip pits, now fishing lakes, dug by Big Brutus is worth the effort for those who make the dizzying 160-foot climb to the top.

A prairie salute to God

Cathedral of the Plains stands out as a monument of faith

No series of Kansas day trips would be complete without a visit to the Cathedral of the Plains, a magnificent structure located at Victoria in eastern Ellis County. And although this powerfully elegant church is, by itself, worth the trip, you should also visit several of the other beautiful churches in the area surrounding Victoria.

If you've traveled on I-70 along the plateau of the Smoky Hills in Ellis County, you've probably seen the mighty spires of St. Fidelis Church, the "cathedral's" real name. The sign on the interstate announces its presence, but this awesome source of considerable local pride must be seen, inside and out, to be fully appreciated.

According to the Rev. Gilmary Tallman, former pastor of St. Fidelis, the church is not officially a cathedral, because cathedrals exist only where a bishop resides. However, when William Jennings Bryan, a 1912 presidential candidate, stopped at Victoria, he was so taken by the church that he called it the Cathedral of the Plains, and the name stuck.

A little history on Victoria and the area around St. Fidelis is necessary to get a feel for why it and other churches were built. According to writings of area historian William Baier, the land surrounding Victoria originally was bought in 1872 by George Grant, a wealthy Scotsman who purchased 80,000 acres from the Kansas Pacific Railroad, the first railroad to cross Kansas.

Grant's intention was to colonize the area with Scotsmen and Britons and build his own Great Plains version of his homeland. He named the city Victoria to honor Queen Victoria of England. His colonists were primarily wealthy young men. In all, 38 men, women and children plus several head of black and red Aberdeen cattle arrived from England in 1873. Baier's written history of the area states that "Victoria became the birthplace of Aberdeen cattle in America."

To make a long story short, Grant died at his ranch house, the "Villa," in April 1878. His ambition of making Victoria a home away from home for his English colonists quickly faded as the gentlemen farmers from across the "water" found pioneer life too different and too difficult. Many chose to return to the more civilized life they enjoyed in England. Grant's home, the "Villa," still stands some five miles south and two miles east of Victoria. In 1972 it was declared a National Historic Site.

In 1876, what was left of Grant's dwindling colony was joined by 23 Volga-German families, folks who chose to flee from their homeland rather than serve in the czar's army in Russia. The Catholic faith, so important in their lives, was being threatened by the czarist regime, so they packed up their religion, families and goods and left Russia to resettle in the Victoria area. There they founded their own village, named Herzog after the village they left on the Volga River in Russia.

Because of their strong religious beliefs, they erected a large wooden cross in the center of the village shortly after their arrival and gathered there on Sundays and evenings to recite the rosary and litanies. Life on the plains however, was incomplete without a church, so in 1876 they celebrated their first Mass in a simple 24-by-40-foot lean-to attached to the home of Aloysius Dreiling.

From 1876 until the dedication of St. Fidelis in 1911, the number of immigrants from Germany, Poland and Russia grew rapidly, making more churches necessary. Bad weather and equally bad roads also made it difficult for churchgoers to travel each Sunday from Walker, Schoenchen (pronounced Shin-shin), Vincent, Munjor, Catherine and Pfeifer to Victoria. As a consequence, churches, many of them magnificent but on a smaller scale than St. Fidelis, were built in those towns and in Ellis, Rush and Barton counties.

Since 1878, the Capuchin Franciscans, originally from Pennsylvania, have ministered to all of the parishes in the area. A monastery for novitiate and ordained friars is adjacent to St. Fidelis.

The Capuchin friars wear distinctive robes with peaked hoods, white knotted sashes (cinctures) and traditional sandals.

About St. Fidelis itself: This incredible example of simple yet striking architecture is testimony to the beauty and strength of native limestone used to its maximum efficiency. The limestone was quarried from the south banks of Big Creek, seven miles south of Victoria near the almost nonexistent community of Vincent. Limestone quarried there is considered some of the finest and richest in the state, according to historian Baier.

Describing the interior of St. Fidelis in this short space would be difficult, but let's just say you'll be impressed by its elegant third century Gothic architecture, highlighted by 45-foot vaulted ceilings and granite pillars quarried in Vermont.

The 14 Stations of the Cross made from hand-carved linden wood and the stained-glass windows are stunning, shining as brightly today as when they were installed in 1916. The windows cost $3,700, and are currently valued by the church's insurance company at $500,000.

Baier frequently gave tours of St. Fidelis until late in 1988. He was a small boy when the church was constructed, but he vividly remembers the laying of its cornerstone in 1906 , and

the dedication in August 1911. Much of the stone used in its construction was quarried from the Baier and Braun family farms on Big Creek.

His firsthand knowledge of the church's construction and background made him the local authority and Victoria's most thorough tour guide. Tallman, when pastor of St. Fidelis, said he would frequently sit in on Baier's tour because he always learned something new and fascinating about the church.

Francis Schippers, Baier's successor, has been conducting lively, entertaining tours of the church since Baier retired. Schippers, like Baier, is a lifelong resident of Victoria and an authority on the history of every church in the area. Groups or individuals interested in arranging tours should call Schippers at (785) 735-2230. The tour's available to all faiths. There is no fee, but donations to St. Fidelis are accepted.

Here are some interesting statistics about St. Fidelis:

The church was built in the shape of a cross facing toward the west.

The main structure is 220 feet long, 110 feet wide and 75 feet high at the nave. The ceiling is 45 feet from the floor. St. Fidelis required 150,000 board feet of lumber. Twenty-three hundred barrels of cement were used, weighing 864,800 pounds.

A prescribed amount of limestone had to be quarried by each family who would eventually attend St. Fidelis. The amount was decided by the number of family members. The height of the twin towers is 141 feet.

There are eight round, six octagonal-shaped and two square solid granite pillars, each measuring 10 feet 10 inches in length. Each pillar weighs 8,500 pounds.

The bells in the towers were installed in 1911. The largest weighs 1,300 pounds, the smallest 275 pounds. They are rung approximately 3,000 times each year.

Dedication services were held August 27, 1911.

The best way to get the most out of your trip to St. Fidelis is to pick up Baier's informative booklet at the church office for a self-guided tour.

Other notable churches in the area are: St. Francis at Munjor, St. Anthony at Schoenchen, St. Joseph at Liebenthal, St. Catherine at Catherine, St. Ann at Walker, St. Mary's at Gorham, St. Boniface at Vincent, St. Ann's at Olmitz and, perhaps the most beautiful of the smaller churches, Holy Cross at Pfeifer.

Many of the churches have closed in recent years. To visit one or more of the churches contact Schippers.

An impressive statue of a Volga German settler, created by artist Pete Felten of Hays, is one of many Felten sculptures in front of and around St. Fidelis Church, also known as the Cathedral of the Plains, in Victoria.

Rolling hills, meandering roads, clear streams and prairie history

The pioneer spirit still exists on the back roads and byways of Chase County

Perhaps my most traveled roads are the ones leading into Chase County, one of the many county jewels dotting the Flint Hills as they undulate from the southern tip of Cowley County to their terminus in north-central Washington County.

My sojourns to Chase County began in 1972 and since that time I have explored virtually every part of this lovely county, a rolling hardwood-dotted landscape where it really isn't all that hard to get lost. But don't get discouraged even if you do get lost. An old friend of mine and a Chase County native admitted to getting lost once, so a newcomer shouldn't feel too bad if your north suddenly turns into a south.

To get there from Doo-Dah, also known as Wichita, take the Kansas Turnpike to Cassoday. Exit there and turn north on K-177. Several miles north of Cassoday, as you make a bend to the north, you'll enter Chase County.

From that point you can toss your "square mile" mentality right out the window, for you are now in the land of twists and turns, hills and valleys — a motorcyclist, bicyclist, hiker and car driver's adventure land on wheels.

With your hair whipping in the wind (you do have your window down, don't you?), glance to your right to watch the masses as they take the mind-numbing turnpike to God-only-knows-where while you begin your adventure across the Great Plains.

Shortly after entering Chase County you may be wondering "Where the heck are the Flint Hills?" You needn't worry — they're right under your wheels, for much like a surfer, you're "hanging ten," riding the crest of an earthen wave that is about to break at your feet.

Not long after you enter Chase County, K-177 drops suddenly from the prairie crest then sweeps you under a railroad trestle, thus beginning a grand prix-like ride through this verdant, undulating landscape.

If you're up for a little back-road adventure right off the bat then watch for mile marker No. 30. Shortly after you see the marker, turn right (east) and take the really roundabout way to Matfield Green.

The first thing you'll come to is a "T" at the Matfield Green cemetery. Make a note of your odometer reading then turn right. From that point always turn left when you get to an intersection and you won't get lost.

About four miles from the cemetery, just after you past over the South Fork of the Cottonwood River, the road turns to gravel, but no matter, it's an all-weather road. (You do have a fully functional spare tire don't you?)

The last house on the left, before you hit the gravel, is the headquarters of Prairie Women Adventures and

Retreat, a 6,000-acre slice of Flint Hills prairie owned by rancher Jane Koger. For information on ranch activities and rates, call (316) 753-3465.

From the beginning of the gravel road you can travel east for 2 3/4 miles, then north to Matfield Green. On the way you'll pass over Cedar Creek shortly before coming to a "T" in the road. Turn left and the road will take you back over the turnpike, then connect with another road where you turn west (left) to Matfield Green.

Another possibility is to travel 6 1/2 miles from the beginning of the gravel road, then turn north (left) for 3 1/2 miles until you hit the main road. From there turn west (left) to Matfield Green.

If you want to visit the highest point in Chase County, travel east for 11 miles from the beginning of the gravel road. Turn left when you get to the prominent relay tower. From there travel about 1 1/2 miles and you'll be pointed into Texaco Hill, 1,637 feet above the plains. It's quite a panoramic view from the top. A group of us once watched what little we could see of Halley's Comet from the crest of that hill.

To remain in Chase County, turn around and head west to one of the two roads that I suggested which will get you back to Matfield Green, or you can take the same road you came in on and it will drop you back at the cemetery, about a mile from Matfield.

When you arrive at Matfield Green you'll be in one of my favorite small towns. When most folks think of Matfield Green they think it's the turnpike gas and food station. In reality it's a small town named for a hamlet in County Kent, England. When David Mercer came to Kansas in 1858, he named the town after the hamlet where he played cricket as a youngster.

It seems only appropriate that the Hitchin' Post, the only "pub" in Matfield Green, is occasionally bartended by Geraldine Wagoner, the former owner of the Hitchin' Post, and a native of Felixstowe, Suffolk County, England. There is no pretense at the Hitchin' Post, only friendly folks, cold beer, soft drinks, and grilled sandwiches. And now they have indoor plumbing. The Hitchin' Post is open Monday through Saturday.

After your visit to Matfield Green you have two excellent options for your journey north. You can drive east from Matfield for six miles, then turn north (left) for a lovely journey to Bazaar on Sharpes Creek Drive.

Or, you can travel north from Matfield on K-177. If you chose the K-177 route you should look to the west (left) as you leave town. On the hillside is a long cinder-block building that once housed train crews. Below the structure are the corrals where, decades ago, cowboys herded cattle onto the

freight cars for delivery to slaughter houses in Kansas City and Chicago.

On down the road a short distance you'll have the opportunity to see and photograph a long stretch of hand-laid limestone fence. The fence leads up to the homestead of Charles Rogler, one of the early settlers in Chase County. Behind the Rogler home, painted on the side of the large white barn behind the Rogler home is "Pioneer Bluffs 1859."

Next to the large home is a replica of the original Rogler family cabin. The bluffs on the west side of the road offer a fine view of the original ranch. The Rogler Ranch continues to operate much as it has since 1859.

And if you're a train buff and you can find a good early morning camera angle on the bluffs, you'll have a number of chances to photograph the dozens of freight trains that pass along the bluffs each day on the way from Chicago to Los Angeles and back.

About four miles past the Rogler Ranch you'll cross a bridge over a single set of railroad tracks. Just past the bridge is a corral, and a mile or so west of the corral is the site of the plane crash that killed Knute Rockne and six other men more than six decades ago. The site is on private land; folks at the Hitchin' Post or at the courthouse in Cottonwood Falls can tell you who to contact to obtain permission to visit the memorial site.

Each April ranchers in Chase County burn off their grasslands to spur new growth of Big and Little Bluestem grasses, the staple diet of the thousands of cattle that are grazed each year in the county.

A few more miles and you're at the turnoff to Bazaar. Take the road to the right and drive into town. Bazaar is another term for marketplace; when it was named that in 1870 it seemed appropriate to the folks from Illinois who settled this Flint Hills community.

The post office closed in 1974, but you can still visit the Post Office Museum in the home of Blanche Schwilling, Bazaar's last postmistress. Call Schwilling at (316) 273-6915 to arrange your visit.

Another icon of Chase County history is the Bazaar United Methodist Church, located at the west edge of town. The church is more than 90 years old and well worth a visit. The door is always open. And yes, the rope hanging just inside the door still rings the bell overhead.

East of Bazaar about a mile is a "T" in the road. Go left to take the back road to Cottonwood Falls or right to venture down Sharpes Creek Drive toward Matfield Green. If you don't have time to take Sharpes Creek Drive all the way to Matfield, then you should at least drive the short distance south of the "T" to visit and photograph the rust-red metal bridge that sits high over the South Fork of the Cottonwood River. It's a pleasant place to stop for a moment and watch the river as it flows toward Cottonwood Falls.

Visitors to the Chase County Courthouse in Cottonwood Falls have the opportunity to climb to the top of the handmade walnut staircase for a view down to the first floor.

An old artillery piece anchors one corner of the square on which sits the Chase County Courthouse, one of the most distinctive county courthouses in Kansas. Built in the 1870s, the structure is Kansas' oldest courthouse in continuous use.

Our next stop is Cottonwood Falls, the Chase County seat. One of the town's most outstanding features is the French Renaissance-style courthouse, reflecting the architectural style of the Louis XIII period. Completed Oct. 8, 1873, it was constructed from hand-cut limestone quarried along the Cottonwood River. It is the oldest Kansas courthouse still in use.

The woodwork inside, including a wonderful spiral staircase, was hand-crafted from walnut trees cut and milled in Chase County. The courthouse stands 113 feet from the ground to the tip of its flagpole. Total construction cost for the project was $42,599.

The courthouse is open for tours weekdays 8 a.m. to 5 p.m., Saturdays, 10 a.m. to 5 p.m., Sundays and holidays, 1 p.m. to 5 p.m. To schedule a tour call (316) 273-6493 or (316) 273-8288. You really need to visit the old jail just to get the feel of cold steel and true discomfort.

Behind the courthouse is the Roniger Memorial Museum. The small building is filled with Indian artifacts collected over the years by brothers Frank and George Roniger. Some of the Ronigers' better finds occurred after the heavy rains in 1951. The Smithsonian wanted the artifacts as part of its American Indian collection, primarily because the items were brought by Indians from other parts of the nation to trade. The Ronigers however, wanted the collection to stay in Chase County. In 1958 they built the Roniger Memorial Museum and dedicated it to their mother, Anna.

North of the courthouse, on the west side of the main street, is the Chase County historical museum, an excellent repository of items donated by Chase County residents. The museum also contains photographs and memorabilia related to the Rockne plane crash site. If you want to know more about the museum, call (316) 273-8500.

During the last decade the folks in Cottonwood Falls, (and from elsewhere), have developed a number of fine businesses in the downtown district including "The Grand Hotel," a first-class overnight stop and eatery. The local folks have also created Bates Grove Park, a fine 7 1/2 acre handicapped accessible picnic area on the northeast side of the Cottonwood Falls dam. The area also offers public fishing access to the Cottonwood River.

The 15-foot tall, 75-yard wide privately-owned dam was originally built of cottonwood logs in 1860. In 1904 it was reconstructed with slabs of cut limestone, then slathered with a thick coat of concrete. Through its history it has provided power for a grist, flour and saw mills, and in 1906 the waters surging through the headrace were used to create electricity. In 1925 the dam served its last commercial purpose as a producer of power for the ice plant adjacent to the river.

Cottonwood Falls and Strong City, just a mile to the north, are known as the "Twin Cities" of Chase County. They were once connected by an interurban track that delivered "Twin Citians" from town to town on horse-drawn rail cars. One remaining rail car is still in use, doing the same kind of task in the Hawaiian islands.

For a real taste of times gone by, plan to attend the Strong City Rodeo during the first weekend in June. The three-day event is one of the largest, most authentic rodeos in Kansas, and the parade and festivities surrounding the rodeo are colorful and entertaining. Bring your camera and take lots of pictures.

Fourteen miles northeast of Strong City is Lake Kahola, a Kansa Indian name meaning "living by the river." The Indian village near where the lake now exists was burned in 1853 because of a smallpox epidemic. Besides being a fine walleye fishery, the 405-acre lake has also served Emporia as an auxiliary water supply since its completion in the 1930s.

Just north of Strong City, on K-177, is Chase County's newest attraction, the Tallgrass Prairie National Preserve, an 11,000-acre swatch of what was the Z-Bar and Spring Hill Ranch. The bulk of ranch is owned by the National Parks Trust, a private, non-profit group dedicated to preserving land for public use. A 160-acre portion of the property is administered by the National Park Service.

Visitors can take self-guided natural history tours across the prairie, from the original homesite to the old Fox Creek School located on a hill to the north. Park rangers and area volunteers also provide guided tours of the magnificent Spring Hill home as well as tram rides through the sprawling grasslands to a lookout point toward the north end of the ranch. For more information about the Tallgrass Prairie National Preserve, call (316) 273-8494.

From the Prairie Preserve I would suggest you travel west from Strong City on U.S. 50 for about three miles or until you cross the railroad tracks. Immediately after the tracks take a right and go about 3/4 mile, then turn right again (north) for an 8 1/2-mile trip to Hymer, or double that to get to Diamond Springs. Don't expect to find a town, as such, when you get to Hymer or Diamond Springs, but do expect a really pleasant drive to get there. It's called Diamond Creek Road, and you can't get lost. The road alternates between being paved and all-weather.

There are a good number of beautiful limestone houses and outbuildings along the road, and you'll see a fine blend of agriculture and pasture land along both sides. It only takes 30 to 45 minutes to get there and you should stop at every bridge to look at Diamond Creek, a lovely little waterway. When you reach either town, turn back and head for U.S. 50.

Our next stop is Elmdale. This place has several great old storefronts. The best time to take pictures is during the morning hours. The limestone city hall building is a 1936 Works Progress Administration project. A couple of doors down is the spruced-up People's Exchange Bank building.

Elmdale is also accessible by way of the Old Cowboy Trail, a good hard-pack road straight west from downtown Cottonwood Falls. The drive from Cottonwood Falls takes you past one of Chase County's hidden treasures, Chase County State Fishing Lake, a jewel of a lake nestled into the Flint Hills. You can't find a nicer place for a break during your day trip, or for a weekend of camping at another time.

From Elmdale take U.S. 50 to the vanishing town of Clements. As you drive into what's left of the town there is an old silver-fronted store facing west. The farm-to-market road south through town will deliver you to the famous Clements bridge.

This double-arch native limestone bridge was built in 1886; its massive twin arches were quarried from both sides of the Cottonwood River it spans. Limestone for the bridge was quarried from the same place as stone for the Chase County Courthouse, the Kansas Capitol, the city auditorium in Topeka, Kansas City's Convention Hall, several buildings at Fort Leavenworth and Fort Riley, as well as for much of the state reformatory at Hutchinson.

It is said to be the largest limestone bridge in Kansas. To tell you the truth, I don't think you'll find a larger or more impressive one. The only odd thing about the bridge is that the dedication plaque was placed on the north side, making it hard to see or photograph.

The farm-to-market road you're on is also the back road to Bazaar. To get to Bazaar drive south from Clements until you have crossed three bridges, and they're all different. Shortly after you cross the third bridge, turn left down a tree-canopied lane tucked up against Coyne Creek. I know it looks like a private drive, but it isn't—trust me.

Take your time and enjoy the tree-shaded drive. If you have a picnic basket then this would be the perfect opportunity to have a quiet, peaceful tailgate lunch. Who knows, you might even see a white-tailed deer or a Rio Grande turkey.

Follow the Coyne Creek road east for about 11 miles through the forest

Wildflowers bloom along the banks of the South Fork of the Cottonwood as it flows south through Chase County. The South Fork empties into the Cottonwood River east of Cottonwood Falls.

and over the hills until it converges with a larger road that continues east to Bazaar.

If you've had all the back-road adventure you can stand forget the Coyne Creek road. From Clements drive 10 miles south, then go two miles east to Wonsevu. This small, virtually unheard of town was founded in 1885, and is said to be named for the Indian word meaning "running deer."

If neither Coyne Creek or Wonsevu are in your plans then continue west on U.S. 50 to Cedar Point. Originally called Cottonwood Valley, Cedar Point was a major trade and social center in the 1870s. Today a bridge leading into town continues to offer a fine view of the Cottonwood River, or you can walk down by the dam where the river's energy once turned the wheels that ground wheat into flour at the old mill on the south side of the dam.

Spring storms and the lighting that accompany them are an integral and fascinating part of living in Kansas.

Beauty in its ruggedness

Chautauqua County, a fine mix of the Osage Questas and the Chautauqua Hills

It's sunrise as we cross into Chautauqua County on K-38. What a fine, beautiful way to start a summer day trip journey. Mourning doves, their bellies filled from feeding, are thick along the power lines while meadowlarks sing their sweet, melodic song.

At the intersection where K-38 runs out we turn right (south), drive a short way, make a dog-leg right, then another back left before crossing over Union Creek, a clear prairie stream bubbling over bedrock on its way to its confluence with the Caney River. It's a fine first look at this county of two landscapes.

One of the most pleasant routes you can travel to experience this rugged and beautiful county is to leave Wichita on K-15, then drive to where it merges with K-38, just east of Winfield. Take K-38 for 13 miles. At that point make the turn toward Union Creek and you'll be at the road south to Cedar Vale. And, as always, drive slowly, roll the windows down and turn off the radio.

Chautauqua County is made up of two distinct geological regions — the Osage Questas and the Chautauqua Hills. The Osage Questas are broad terraces of prairie. Imagine yourself standing on a hill overlooking a beautiful expanse of undulating landscape — a sweeping panorama that touches the soul. It's the stuff of Kansas, pure prairie, pure poetry.

As you drive south you'll be on a wonderful drive to Cedar Vale, the Osage Questas town named for the trees that abound in the area. A few miles north of town you'll cross an old metal bridge spanning Otter Creek, another feeder of the Caney River. Pull to the side of the road and stop for a moment to enjoy this stream as it rushes into a pool teeming with catfish and spotted bass.

Cedar Vale is a peaceful little community, but it can't be properly appreciated if you blast through on U.S. 166 as it passes through town east-to-west. Take the time to explore the downtown and residential areas to the north and south of the highway. Directly under the water tower is a nice park for the kids.

From the west edge of town take the road south to Hewins. The Hewins Road will be the first road south as you enter Cedar Vale from the west on U.S. 166. Stop at the convenience store on the west edge of town and ask directions to Hewins and to the "Wee Kirk in the Valley."

The "Wee Kirk" is, as the name implies, a small church about five miles southwest of Cedar Vale. Built more than 25 years ago by Lotus Day of rural Cedar Vale, the chapel measures 8 by 14 feet. Six pews made of eastern oak were designed by Day to be just large enough to seat Christ and his 12 disci-

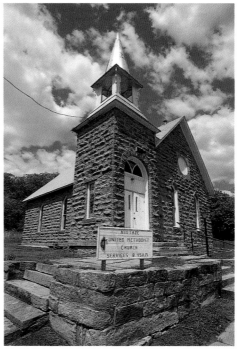

Located south of Cedarvale, the Wee Kirk in the Valley is open to visitors 365 days a year. Built by Lotus M. Day, the 12-seat chapel opened to visitors in 1964. In front of the chapel is a six-foot white carrara marble statue of Christ.

The interior of the Wee Kirk in the Valley. The six two-seat pews made of eastern oak represent seating for the 12 disciples of Christ.

The limestone First United Methodist Church is one of the landmarks in the small town of Niotaze.

ples. It's an interesting piece of Americana, something to visit and photograph on your way to Hewins.

The road continues south then east, then south, then east and so on until you get to the very small town of Hewins. This is a magnificent drive through rolling prairie and blackjack oak forests. You'll pass over a number of metal bridges spanning Caney River tributaries until about a mile before town, where you cross the Caney itself. Be sure to stop for a look at each creek crossing, but pull over to the side of the road so others can pass.

Hewins, named for rancher and politician Edwin Hewins, is about done save for the Church of Christ on the west edge of town. Several families call Hewins home, but economically the town has ceased to exist. Historically, rancher Hewins was once involved in a county seat fight that lead to what was then called Howard County, being divided into Elk and Chautauqua counties.

From Hewins take the popular scenic drive to Elgin. Two and a half miles east of Hewins there once stood a rusty metal bridge (Hart's Mill) over the Caney River. It was removed and replaced in the late 1980s. Find a place to stop and photograph one of the most popular and productive catfish rivers in southeast Kansas.

The road between Hewins and Elgin is one that you should definitely put on your top 20 list of delightful drives in Kansas. Slow down and enjoy the drive, and never hesitate to take one of the side roads down to the river. The county map or the DeLorme Atlas and Gazetteer will correctly guide you along your journey beside the Caney River. At one point on the trip to Elgin you will parallel the Kansas-Oklahoma border.

History has it that Rome Hanks, blood kin to Nancy Hanks Lincoln, settled in Elgin and was appointed postmaster in 1871 by President Ulysses S. Grant. Hanks built a small hotel and a stone building that later became a church. The hotel is gone and the church building is used for storage. Hanks is buried in the Elgin cemetery.

In 1866 the railroad came to Elgin, an act that enabled Elgin to become a very large shipping point for cattle herded up from Texas. From 1890 until 1910 Elgin claimed to be the largest cattle terminal in the world, loading more than 6,000 carloads in 1902.

At its peak Elgin had 2,300 residents, five general stores, nine saloons, a newspaper, a bank, two doctors, an undertaker and a variety of other businesses including female companionship for trail-weary cowboys. The old wooden bridge over the Caney River proved to be a popular spot for hanging cattle rustlers and other undesirables.

Elgin, if you believe the old sign in front of Margaret's Cafe, is "A Town Too Tough to Die." The town's original name was Hudson, but no one there seems to recall why it was changed to Elgin. Elgin is a Scottish name that was used fairly commonly to name towns born in the 1800s.

Now all that's left of are a few businesses, a mechanic and Margaret's Cafe. In 1988, when I asked Margaret Brin, owner of the cafe, if the "too-tough-to-die" sign was right, she just smiled and said, "Yep!"

The walls of Margaret's Cafe are a nice catchall of old and new photographs of giant catfish taken from the Caney River, yellowed newspaper clippings, a canceled check from a Sedan bank dated in the 1890s and an assortment of other oddities. If it's open, stop at Margaret's and catch up on what's going on in and around Elgin.

If you like to hunt or fish, Cedar Creek and scattered tracts of the 844-acre Hulah Wildlife Area are located just to the northeast of Elgin.

As you leave Elgin driving east toward the town of Chautauqua, you are leaving the Osage Questas and entering the widest portion of the Chautauqua Hills region. According to the map produced by the Kansas Department of Transportation, "This (physiographic) province is only a few miles wide. The underlying rock is thick sandstone." In other words, it looks different and it's cut a little rougher than the Osage Questas you've been traveling through. The difference is subtle, but discernible, if you slow down and pay attention to the changes in terrain.

From Chautauqua, a town that takes its name from a Seneca Indian word related to fishing, you have several options. You can travel north to Sedan and Peru or you can take the Sand Hill Road east to the 2,360-acre Copan Wildlife Area, located just west of Caney. Bring your camera — there are plenty of critters to photograph if you're there toward sunset.

Until the early 1990s, travelers were able to drive through Peru on U.S. 166, but since the state rerouted the highway you need to make a special effort to see the downtown. Peru was named by a fellow by the name of E.R. Cutler. Cutler's hometown was Peru, Illinois. On the east edge of town are the walled remnants of an old brick factory.

If you decided to visit the Copan Wildlife Area you should angle north to Niotaze (pronounced NEY-o-taz), a town originally called Jay Hawk, but later, for reasons no one can remember, it was changed to Matanzas, Spanish for "massacre." Sixteen years later it was changed to Niota, a word of Siouan origin.

It was changed one last time by the postmaster who added the appendage "ze" to avoid any possible confusion with the town of Neola in Labette County. Neola later ceased to exist. Niotaze is the only town in the United States with that name. Historian John Rydjord noted in "Indian Place-Names" that "While this name is sufficiently distinctive, it is also meaningless."

Stop at the post office to get the lowdown on how the town was named. Several years ago the Niotazians tired of their old concrete, bunker-style city hall and built a new one. You can still see the old city hall from the highway. It sits 35 yards west of the new building. Quite an improvement, I'd say.

A good back-road drive from Niotaze starts about a mile east of town on U.S. 166. The road takes you north through the hills and drops you into Sedan, the Chautauqua County seat.

Sedan, named for a town in France, is the birthplace of the clown Emmett Kelly, and is home of the Sedan Blue Devils and the Yellow Brick Road. The Emmett Kelly Museum is on the north side of U.S. 166. Museum hours are: Monday through Friday 10 a.m. to noon and 1 p.m. to 5 p.m., Sunday 1 p.m. to 5 p.m. For special appointments, call (316) 725-3470.

The Yellow Brick Road is the brainchild of Nita Jones of Sedan. For $15 you or your family can have his or her name stamped in a semi-immortal 8 by 12-inch brick of yellowish concrete. Four-by-four foot sections of these bricks fill the downtown sidewalks of Sedan. So far more than 10,000 folks have joined the ranks of solid citizens lining the sidewalks of Sedan.

Drive the streets of Sedan. There are many beautiful old homes and a number of fine shops and good places to eat. The city park on the north end of town is a nice spot for a picnic.

Speaking of picnics, you really ought to take in the Sedan City Lakes just north of town on K-99. At both lakes you can fish, picnic or hike in relative seclusion. And there isn't much "people pressure" on the weekends, either.

Take your time and enjoy the unusual blend of geology in Chautauqua County. The clear streams, abundant wildlife, oak forests and massive rock formations are delightful and photogenic. And the small towns along the way are well worth a visit.

Council Grove, the last pit stop before Santa Fe

In Council Grove, history takes a front seat all over town

Kansas and the opening of the West are inseparable. In the early 1800s Kansas was a major staging area for our nation's westward movement. And no city in Kansas has more evidence of the pioneer movement than Council Grove.

Thirty-seven miles south of Manhattan at the junction of K-177 and U.S. 56, Council Grove, the Morris County seat, sits smack-dab at the crossroads of the Prairie Parkway and the Santa Fe Trail, and has 18 historical sites.

It's easy to fill a day or two at Council Grove, especially if you visit there during the annual Wah-Shun-Gah Days celebration the second weekend of each June. The annual party has a pow-wow, parade, carnival and craft show. And the new river walk at the east end of the business district will give visitors a close look at the Neosho River as it flows through town.

One place that should encourage you to stay the night in Council Grove is the Cottage House Hotel, a beautiful two-story brick building built in 1867 as a three-room cottage and blacksmith shop. The building was added on to through the years. The Queen Anne style addition is the most elegant portion of the building. The rooms must be stayed in to be appreciated.

Consider these sight-seeing options: Council Grove Oak, Custer Elm, Post Office Oak, the Last Chance Store, the Kaw Mission, the Hays House, Hermit's Cave, Council Grove Bell, Pioneer Jail, Madonna of the Trail, and the Old Stone Barn. That's the list, now let's go over some of the particulars.

Council Grove has three historic trees. Two of the trees, Council Grove Oak and Custer Elm, are dead and sheltered for posterity, but Post Office Oak continues to hang on to life.

The most historic of the three trees is the Council Grove Oak, so named because of the treaty signed between U.S. government representative George Sibley and 50 chiefs and warriors of the Great and Small Osage tribes on Aug. 10, 1825.

The Neosho River, along the southern edge of Council Grove, was once the last large stand of hardwood trees between there and Santa Fe, N.M. It was "one of the last wooded areas where folks could cut axle trees for their wagons before journeying on to Santa Fe," said Larry Jochims, Kansas State Historical Society researcher.

With the signing of the treaty, the West was officially opened for trade and settlement along what was originally known as the Santa Fe Road. The Santa Fe Trail was one of commerce more than anything else.

The Custer Elm is named for the ill-fated general who was perhaps the first man to know the true meaning of wearing an "arrow" shirt. The elm was the centerpiece of his favorite site when he and his troops from Fort Riley camped along Elm Creek. Custer liked the area so much he bought 120 acres of land. The unsubstantiated rumor was that Custer intended to settle in the area when he retired. The Sioux, however, had other plans for Custer at a place called Little Big Horn.

The last, and most interesting, tree is the Post Office Oak, said to be at least 175 years old. Westbound pioneers would leave letters at its base under a pile of rocks. Folks bound for the East would pick them up, thus creating an informal mailing system that endured from 1825 to 1847.

Take a few moments to sit under the history-laden branches of this fine tree. Close your eyes and listen as the wind whispers tales of yesteryear.

The Last Chance Store: Think about the meaning of that name, because in 1857 when the store was built, folks didn't kid about such things. In fact, there were only two small trading posts on stream crossings located to the west of Council Grove, and they didn't have that much to offer. The traders who left Council Grove had seven hundred miles of backbreaking work ahead of them with virtually no opportunity to pick up another ox, axle or loaf of bread.

Whenever you feel like whining about the inconvenience of having to go to the store to get this or that, think about how it used to be on the trail when Council Grove's Last Chance Store, as well as two other larger general stores, were the only sizable pit stops in the territory. Today the original building houses an antique store.

The Kaw Mission was built by the U.S. government in 1847 as a school for the Kaw, or Kansa Indians. According to a local tour guide, the government thought the Indians ought to be educated, but the Indians disagreed. It didn't last long as an Indian school. It later became one of the first schools for white children in Kansas.

The government not only thought Indians should be educated, it thought they should live in stone houses on the reservation. The Indians preferred to live outside and put their horses in the houses. One story was that the houses had square corners, and the Indians, who normally lived in round hogans, thought the corners were evil.

In 1873 the government moved the Kaw to their present home in Oklahoma. The Kaw Mission is administered by the Kansas State Historical Society. For information, call (316) 767-5410.

The Hays House, built by Seth Hays in 1847 as a trading post, was enlarged in 1857 and has been used continuously as a restaurant since that time. Hays, great-grandson of Daniel Boone and cousin of Kit Carson, was the first white man to settle in Council Grove. Through the early years, the Hays House functioned as a post office, theater, church, newspaper office and home for U.S. court hearings. Today it is regarded as one of the finest dining establishments in the state.

Hermit's Cave is a favorite spot for youngsters to visit. It isn't exactly a cave — it's more of a niche — so don't expect to walk into the side of a hill. But, in the early 1860s, it was the home for a short time of an Italian named Giovanni Maria Augustini, a religious mystic who had problems getting along with folks just about everywhere he went. Augustini's so-called cave was an alcove under a shelf of rock on the side of what is now known as Belfrey Hill.

During his five-month residence in Council Grove, he worked with the Kaw Indians. They soon tired of the religious fanatic and suggested he take a hike, and make it a long one. Feeling unwelcome, Augustini left Council Grove for a new home on a mountainside, now known as Hermit's Peak near Las Vegas, N.M. He was eventually killed by Indians in southern New Mexico.

The Council Grove Bell was poured in 1863 for a church in Lawrence, but the bell had a defect. A Council Grove publisher named Sam Woods heard about the bell, bought it and hauled it back to Council Grove, where he put it on a hill for use as a local communications system.

It rang for church, school, fires, weddings, floods and Indian raids, although no one seems to remember the various ring codes. The bell is on Belfrey Street on Belfrey Hill.

Pioneer Jail was the first and only jail in the early days of the Santa Fe Trail and was originally called a calaboose. It was two stories high, with the sheriff or jailer living on the second floor. The second story rotted off a long time ago.

The Madonna of the Trail monument was placed in Council Grove by the Daughters of the American Revolution in 1928 and commemorates National Old Trails Road. According to local historians, the U.S. government would sanction a survey for an official road to accommodate westward expansion. The Santa Fe Trail became a segment of that series of roads running from the East Coast into California. This continuation of roadways became known as the National Old Trails Road. It passes through 12 states, and there is a Madonna in each state. They all face west and are identical.

Another feature worth visiting is the Old Stone Barn, located about one mile east of Council Grove on the north side of the highway. The barn, currently being restored, was built in 1871 on land owned by Hays. The 76-foot long stone building is the only remaining vestige of the Morris County Poor Farm that existed there from 1889-1945.

If you haven't had enough fun visiting all these wonderful vestiges of the past, then take K-177 north for five miles to the Council Grove Reservoir. The reservoir is open to picnicking, fishing, boating or you can swim to break up the day's visit. The reservoir has 3,280 surface acres and 40 miles of shoreline for wandering. You'll also find a fine fishing hole at Council Grove City Lake, located about five miles west of the dam. There is a fee to fish the lake and if you're looking for a summer home there are always a number of cottages for sale at the lake.

For information about group or guided tours, call the Council Grove Chamber of Commerce at (800) 732-9211.

Did You Know?

How often were horses changed in the Pony Express?
Every 10 to 15 miles

What railway was known as the "Look, Cuss and Wait"?
Leavenworth, Kansas and Western

Where did Coronado enter Kansas?
Near Liberal in Seward County

Zebulon Pike's expedition entered Kansas in September 1806 near what present-day town?
Fort Scott in Bourbon County

Who is credited with being the first Kansan to promote the statewide use of hard red winter wheat?
Bernhard Warkentin of Newton in Harvey County

What Kansan was known as the "Horse and Buggy Doctor"?
Arthur Hertzler of Halstead in Harvey County

Where was the first public-use bathtub in Kansas?
Ames Hotel, Wamego in Pottawatomie County

When Buffalo Bill Cody was a Pinkerton agent, what county was his headquarters?
Cowley County

The symbol Jayhawk was created from what two birds?
The bluejay and the kestrel

For what two Kansas brothers was McConnell Air Force Base named?
Tom and Fred

Which wing of the Kansas Capitol was erected first?
The east

How many miles are in the Kansas Turnpike?
233

On Oct. 25, 1864, a Civil War battle was fought in Kansas. Name the battle.
Battle of Mine Creek (Linn County)

What royalty visited Lindsborg in 1976?
King Carl Gustaf of Sweden

What Kansas community was called the Broomcorn Capital of the World?
McPherson in McPherson County

What Delphos resident persuaded Lincoln to grow a beard?
Grace Bedell

How many states have the meadowlark as the state bird?
Six: Kansas, Montana, Nebraska, North Dakota, Oregon, Wyoming

What is a pound party?
It's the old-time custom of taking foodstuffs to new people in a community, particularly ministers

Born in Manhattan in 1884, he became a reporter and short-story writer, and his name was given to a famous cancer fund. Who was he?
Damon Runyon

Who was the first native Kansan to appear on a U.S. postage stamp?
William Allen White

Who was the first Kansan into space?
Ronald Evans of St. Francis in Cheyenne County.

Where is the state flower shown on the flag of Kansas?
Above the seal

The great, untainted outdoors... and then some

Cowley County is a perfect place to spend the day exploring nature and history

Cowley County is truly a back road driver's delight, but take it slow and stop often.

The roads are good, and what you'll see along the way is easy on the eyes and soothing to the soul. We'll talk about some towns on this trip, but mostly we'll visit the hills and back roads of this, the most southern region of the Flint Hills.

Take the Kansas Turnpike south from Wichita to the U.S. 166 exit, certainly one of the top 20 scenic highways in Kansas. Shortly before you arrive at Arkansas City you'll see a sign directing you north to the Chaplin Nature Center, a sweet slice of prairie along the Arkansas River. The area is owned and managed by the Wichita Audubon Society.

What you'll find at Chaplin are hundreds of acres of pure, natural prairie bordered by a wide stretch of the Arkansas. The Center offers everything from river views to canopied woodlands to rolling prairie, and the unique variety of wildlife that live in those ecosystems. What makes the area even more special is the first-class interpretative center.

The Chaplin Nature Center has a full-time, on-site manager and naturalist, and provides visitors with an up-close and personal look at nature's wonders. Everything is free, although donations are encouraged. It's a delightful experience for anyone interested in learning about prairie ecosystems and an excellent place to educate young people about life in the wild. If you have questions about the center or want to know about future programs, call (316) 442-7227 or (316) 442-4133.

Arkansas City, situated on a bluff overlooking the confluence of the Arkansas and Walnut rivers, is a fine place to visit. It was originally called Walnut City, then Adelphi, then Creswell, before city officials finally settled on Arkansas City in 1872. They probably couldn't afford to keep changing the signs.

One particularly attractive and extraordinary limestone building in Arkansas City is the old high school, constructed in 1890. The stone was quarried at Silverdale, east of Arkansas City. It's on Second Street, one block west of Main Street. Be sure to drive the length of Main Street, and take a good look around the town. You won't be disappointed.

The Chamber of Commerce, at 126 E. Washington, is open Monday through Friday, 8 a.m. to 5 p.m. Inside the Chamber of Commerce is a wall full of brochures with information about local points of interest and events in the area. Call (316) 442-0230 and ask them to send you a packet of local information.

When you leave Arkansas City drive east on U.S. 166 to the

*Surprised by a passerby, a white-tailed doe, alfalfa
dangling from her mouth, bounds toward the
safety of the woods.*

Silverdale/Maple City road. Watch for the sign — it's easy to miss because U.S. 166 makes a sharp turn north right where you're supposed to get off the highway for Silverdale. At that point you'll turn south.

At the south edge of Silverdale is the H.J. Born Stone Co., the company where much of the construction limestone in Kansas is sliced and diced. From Silverdale continue south and enjoy the beautiful valley of Grouse Creek, named for the wild grouse (greater prairie chickens) that abound in the surrounding Flint Hills. Kansans can proudly boast that we have the largest population of prairie chickens in the United States.

During the spring, male prairie chickens put on extravagant mating displays on traditional "booming grounds." The males tilt their bodies forward, their tail feathers fanned out, and orange air sacs inflated as their ears point skyward in an effort to attract a mate.

You'll cross over Grouse Creek three times before traveling up a hill. On the hilltop is a fine panoramic view of the valley to the north. You're in the heart of the 4,300-acre KAW Wildlife Area, one of the few places in Kansas where anglers and canoeists have excellent public access to a scenic waterway, specifically Grouse Creek.

Toward the top of the hill, a paved road cuts back to the west, then winds down through the woods to a public boat ramp where you can put in at the point where Grouse Creek feeds into the Arkansas River. From there you can go upstream for several miles or head down the Arkansas River to the Mississippi River. It's all public water from the boat ramp south to the Gulf of Mexico.

After enjoying the hilltop view, turn around and take the road back toward Silverdale. After crossing the creek once take the first road left (west) for a back-road trip that will return you to the Silverdale road about two miles east of town. It's a pleasant twist and turn drive lined with a wide variety of flowering plants. Don't forget to bring your camera and color film.

As you drive east from Silverdale you might see a macabre scenario on the right side of the road. The things adorning the tops of fence posts are the heads of large catfish taken from nearby Grouse Creek. If the fence-top decorations are good indicators, I'd say fishing around these parts is mighty productive.

If you go right back to Silverdale, then take the road north for about two miles to U.S. 166. From there travel east on U.S. 166 for 2 1/4 miles, then take the gravel road north as it follows Grouse Creek to Dexter.

I know the road looks iffy, maybe even untraveled, but it's an excellent back-road drive of about nine or 10 miles. Don't be deterred by the lack of traffic, or by its resemblance to a private drive — it isn't. It's just a sign that you have the road to yourself and are about to have wonderful prairie experience instead of dodging traffic on U.S. 166 and K-15. Use a Cowley County map or the DeLorme Atlas to guide you to Dexter.

Dexter is the home of Henry's Candy Co., and, as luck would have it, Henry's is open seven days a week from 8 a.m. to 5 p.m. Stop in and watch candy being produced and eaten right before your eyes.

This small Flint Hills community has two other distinctions. Helium was discovered in Dexter in 1903, and the town was named after Dexter, a well-known racehorse in the 1870s. A town named for a racehorse is a nice change of pace from towns and counties being named for Civil War veterans. Cowley County, coincidentally, was named for Lt. Matthew Cowley of the 9th Kansas Infantry, who died during a battle at Little Rock in 1864.

From Dexter take K-15 north to where it intersects with K-38. Then turn right and go one mile, then go north for five miles, then right (east) to Cambridge, named for the well-known English university. From Cambridge you have two good options. You can travel north for a pleasant eight-mile drive to the road west to Atlanta and Rock or you can take the first road right (south) and travel for five miles until you hook back up with K-38. This drive takes you above and through Grouse Creek valley, and I highly recommend it. When you're finished with the Grouse Creek drive, take K-38 west until it becomes K-15 again and continue west to where K-15 and U.S. 160 become one, about six miles.

Before you turn south at that point you might want to take a five to six-mile trip north to visit New Salem. It was platted in only 12 square blocks in 1882, kind of small compared to most towns developed during that period. I guess the city fathers didn't have high hopes that New Salem would be a metropolis of any real importance.

Worth seeing in New Salem is the old public water supply well on the main street. It's a canopied affair with a peaked front decorated with sealed-in-glass portraits of early-day city officials.

Back on U.S. 160 where it blends with K-15, turn left (south) on the blacktop toward Silverdale. At the Rose Valley Cemetery turn right (west) for a pleasant drive to Winfield, the Cowley County seat on the confluence of Walnut and Timber creeks.

Named for Winfield Scott, a Baptist preacher from Leavenworth, this fine Flint Hills town has taken full advantage of the limestone quarried nearby.

Many of the downtown buildings reflect the beauty of the county's rock-solid foundation. Built in 1962, the county courthouse, constructed from Silverdale limestone, has a 20-foot county map carved into the smooth surface. Each township and town is represented as well as the major creeks and rivers.

The Cowley County museum, 1011 Mansfield, is housed in the old Bryant School built in 1886. It's a simple limestone structure and one of Winfield's original school buildings. The museum offers a good look into the history of Cowley County through displays of area artifacts and exhibits. It's open weekends from 2 to 5 p.m. Admission is free.

On the north end of town is Island Park Lake, a pleasant, tree-canopied city park built on an island surrounded by Timber Creek. There's plenty of things to keep the youngsters busy and loads of picnic areas. It's a good place to fish or to kick back and rest a spell on a fine Kansas day. And at Christmas the local folks fill the park with thousands of Christmas lights.

Three miles east and about six miles north of town is Winfield City Lake. It has just about anything you need to have a good outdoor experience. You can swim, fish, water-ski or camp, and during waterfowl season you're allowed to down a duck or two. All other hunting is prohibited at the lake.

Timber Creek marina, (316) 221-6731, on the south side of the lake near the dam has food, fuel, boating supplies and bait. The lake's 1,200 surface acres and 21 miles of shoreline offer a pleasant variety of outdoor experiences.

If you're in Winfield in September then you'll be in for quite a treat. Flat pickers and bluegrass singers from across the United States converge on the banks of the Walnut River for the Walnut Valley Festival, also known as the National Guitar Flat-Picking Championships. The event is held at the Winfield fairgrounds, next to U.S. 160 on the west edge of town.

If you've ever wondered where all the hippies went, then show up for the festival and you'll see 'em all over the place. For the most part their hair is shorter and grayer, and their waistlines larger, but they'll be there in force with their kids and grandkids. You can count on the Walnut Valley Festival to be one of the finest outdoor events in Kansas each year.

The land of some famous firsts

A sculpted beauty, Doniphan County remains unknown to most Kansans

Doniphan County. It's the historic corner of Kansas everyone is familiar with but knows little about. It's the place where Kansas began, where settlers from Illinois, Ohio, Iowa and Indiana set down their roots to foster the first generations of Kansans in this glaciated region sometimes referred to as "Little Switzerland."

Established Aug. 25, 1855, it was the first county in Kansas to have a name. It took its name from Alexander W. Doniphan, a Missourian who was a colonel in the Mexican-American War of 1846. Doniphan's cavalry unit took a prominent role in the conquest of New Mexico, and he was a zealot in his efforts to extend slavery into Kansas.

From the air, the landscape of Doniphan County looks as if it were sculpted by giant fingers twisting and turning through sand. In geological terms the very deep top layer of this wooded and rolling landscape is called loess — fine ground, fertile soil up to several hundred feet thick in places. In aesthetic terms the landscape is serene and inviting.

Doniphan County is a fairly long haul from just about everywhere. If you live in Wichita, about 190 miles to the southwest, you would need to leave home at 4 a.m. From Wichita, take the Kansas Turnpike to Topeka, get off and find U.S. 24 at the northeast corner of Topeka.

Once on U.S. 24, drive a short distance east then take K-4 north past Meridan, Valley Falls, Nortonville and on up to Atchison.

If you don't want to do the early morning thing, you can drive up the afternoon before and spend the night in Atchison. The important thing is to start your Doniphan County day trip as the sun rises from the fog covering the Missouri River. It's worth the extra effort.

From Atchison drive north on K-7. It's a fine roller coaster ride through a delightful landscape fashioned by wind and time. Your destination is Troy, the Doniphan County seat. It was named for its Greek counterpart by J.R. Whitehead, the county clerk.

There's something very comfortable about Troy. Perhaps it's the town square with its rustic and beautiful county courthouse flanked by a maple tree that glows flame-orange in the fall. Or maybe it's the friendly crowd across the street at Sheila's Restaurant where hot biscuits and gravy are sure to hit the spot on just about any morning.

Doniphan County's brick courthouse was built in 1906 and has a unique feature on its south lawn: a 35-foot burr oak sculpture of a Plains Indian. The Peter Toth original is his 29th such creation in as many states and weighs in the neighborhood of eight to 10 tons. Toth has produced similar sculptures in all 50 states, as well as several in Canada.

In the 1930s Troy was a major shipping point for apples grown on more than 10,000 acres of local orchards. The orchards have diminished in size, but there are many parts of Doniphan County that continue to produce large quantities of fruits and vegetables.

Just a couple of doors down from Sheila's is the Kansas Chief, a hometown weekly that's also the oldest newspaper in Kansas. News in the Kansas Chief revolves around community events, the high school football, basketball or track team achievements, high school homecoming king and queen candidates or a story about the new farm implement dealer.

Everything in the Chief is dedicated to local news for local readers, an interesting concept in a time when newspapers cater to fanciful facts, gossip, colorful photos, graphics, and the "news you can use" concept. Take some time to drive the streets of Troy. It has the feel of a Norman Rockwell painting with a touch of Edward Hopper light at the right time of day. If you don't know who those artists are, then you need to brush up on great American painters.

Driving west from Troy on U.S. 36 you'll find crops of soybeans, milo and feed corn, the primary crops in Doniphan County. During the fall those fields take on a golden hue as the crops ripen under an autumn sun. A mile or two before Highland is a sign

St. Joseph's Catholic Church sits atop a hill overlooking downtown Wathena. Wathena was named for a Kickapoo Indian chief.

The picturesque Doniphan County Courthouse, located in Troy, sits squarely in the middle of the town square, surrounded by the business district. The Indian sculpture was created from a single burr oak tree by artist Peter Toth.

directing you to the Iowa, Sac and Fox Indian Mission next to Mission Creek.

You should visit the mission, established by Presbyterians in 1837. This starkly attractive three-story building was built as a classroom, chapel and dormitory. The Iowa, Sac and Fox tribes' lack of interest in education and religion combined with withering epidemics caused the mission to close in the 1860s.

The recently refurbished building now serves as a repository of artifacts, including original furniture, clothes and a fine selection of Indian points and bead and leather work on the third floor. On the second floor is the church, an interesting and fundamental part of the mission. Outside, tree-shaded picnic grounds surround the mission, making it a perfect place to stop and reflect on the history of this area.

Today the Iowa, Sac and Fox Reservation covers approximately 30 square miles in northeastern Brown County, northern Doniphan County and southeastern Richardson County, Nebraska.

At Highland is Highland Junior College, the oldest college in Kansas. Originally known as Highland University, it was established in 1858, three years before Kansas became a state. Irvin Hall, the original building on campus, continues to serve the student body, and is Kansas' oldest higher-education building in continuous use.

One other interesting note about the college is that it accepted George Washington Carver as a student and then, for racial reasons, had second thoughts about his admission. College administrators rejected Carver when he showed up for classes.

Highland takes its name not from its geological vantage point, but from a namesake town in Illinois.

From Highland take U.S. 36 west for about a mile to where the road bends south next to a small roadside park. From there take the road north for another rural view of Doniphan County on your way to White Cloud.

Named for James White Cloud, (Mahaska), chief of the Prairie Sioux, the town was organized by Dr. Richard Gatling, among others, in 1857. He later invented the famous Gatling gun. This, the northeastern most community of Kansas, holds a unique place in our state's history.

In the 1850s White Cloud was a wild and woolly frontier town on the banks of the Missouri River. For many it was the last view of civilized living before they headed into the western wilderness. Steamboats regularly docked at White Cloud, where they dumped their cargoes of settlers, goods, hooligans and livestock. Saloons thick with riverboat gamblers, Southern belles and wide-eyed Easterners made White Cloud the place to be in the 1850s.

The Kansas Chief newspaper originated in White Cloud until a declining economy in 1873 caused its move to Troy.

A national institution of sorts had its start in White Cloud in the early 1900s when a local boy, Walter Chapman, sold his pig to raise money to help a youngster at a leper colony in Louisiana. Chapman's deed gained national attention through several newspaper stories and before long, small pig-shaped objects began appearing on store shelves. The generous boy from White Cloud had inspired the piggy bank.

By Kansas standards, White Cloud is a hilly community. On a prominence north of town you can see four states. Part of the view is of the Missouri River as it snakes into Kansas from the north. The river is very much a part of the life and history of Doniphan County. It sculpts a distinctive, meandering shape along the eastern edge of Doniphan, Atchison, Leavenworth and Wyandotte counties before turning into Missouri. Take a short drive north along the river for a turnaround visit to Nebraska.

Perhaps the most famous character in White Cloud is "Wolf River" Bob Breeze.

Breeze grew up in White Cloud, then moved to California where he was a stunt man in a number of motion pictures. Drawn home by his Kansas roots, Breeze has become the area's number one showman and promoter.

His 200-acre hilltop view of the Missouri River is known as Lewis and Clark Lookout. For a very small price Breeze allows campers and other folks to use the area for social events, weddings, campouts and the like. It's a wonderful place to visit, particularly if you're fond of an outdoor experience, and that, of course, includes the outhouse.

White Cloud also puts on a community buffet every Sunday at the VFW on the east edge of town, about a block from the Missouri River. The door is always open, cost is minimal, the folks are friendly and the food is great. And, if you're in White Cloud on the first Sunday in May or September you'll be up to your eyes with the 10,000 to 15,000 folks who attend the huge flea market held there twice each year.

Southeast on K-7 takes you back to Sparks, where K-7 and U.S. 36 intersect. Just before Sparks is the road east to Eagle Springs. Once a mineral watering hole for the rich, this former resort area is now on private grounds. A nice backroad drive near there starts about 1 1/2 miles before Sparks.

You'll know you're on the right track if you cross a bridge immediately after leaving K-7. The road travels northeast across the hills and eventually takes you back to U.S. 36 south of Sparks. If you're in doubt about what road to take, stop in Sparks; anyone there

can give you directions.

Just north of Sparks is Lookout Mountain, one of the highest hills in Kansas, more than 350 feet above the banks of the Missouri River. Between Troy and Wathena is Blair, elevation 900 feet. I mention it only because of the huge fruit and vegetable stand there that displays all manner of good things to eat from first summer harvest through fall.

Wathena, named for the Kickapoo chief who allowed settlers to hold church services in his wigwam, is a fine little town in the middle of apple-growing country. The downtown is a short distance off the highway to the west. Take the time to drive through and visit the impressive St. Joseph's Catholic Church on the hill overlooking town.

From the south side of the church drive southwest on the road to Palermo. At that point you can take any number of roads west to K-7 or test your navigation skills and find your way along the river to the disappearing town of Doniphan, in the southeast corner of the county.

Doniphan, the county namesake, was the home of a large Kansa Indian village in 1675. Named for Alexander Doniphan, the Mexican War guy, it was once a bustling river town of more than 2,000 and an important part of Missouri River activity in the 1850s.

Kansas' first grain elevator was built

in Doniphan, a 100-acre vineyard produced millions of gallons of wine around the turn of the century and as many as 20 steamboats docked at the Doniphan wharf each day. But as time passed Atchison grew to river prominence, and the economy of Doniphan declined, causing many businesses to move to more financially rewarding areas in the county.

The railroad, a vital economic link, was washed away in a flood and rebuilt farther away from town. That pretty much did it for Doniphan. All that's left today is a scattering of homes and the ruins of a general store.

Take the time to find your way along the Missouri from Palermo to Doniphan and be sure to stop along the banks and imagine what it was like to watch a steamboat, lighted only by candlelight and coal oil, as it pushed upriver silhouetted against a twilight sky.

Of trees and battles and a historic railroad

In all seasons, Douglas County is rich in what attracts visitors

Pound for pound, it's hard to find a place with more Kansas history than Douglas County. Add the history to a breathtaking mixture of Osage Questas, and glaciated geology and you've got a beautiful, successful day trip in your immediate future. Let's do it!

Take the Kansas Turnpike from Wichita to Emporia, get on I-35 to Ottawa, then take U.S. 59 north for about 10 miles and you're there.

Now, wasn't that easy?

Just a mile into the county you'll pass an old motel on the left side of the road. It sits on a slight uphill grade, the rooms stacked end-to-end, staircase style. It's a nice slice of our past for those who remember when motels were cheaper, less fancy, more functional and perhaps more down-to-earth.

At the intersection of U.S. 59 and U.S. 56 turn right (east) to Baldwin City, home of the Maple Leaf Festival on the third weekend of each October.

About three miles before Baldwin City you'll pass near the site of the Battle of Black Jack, fought June 2, 1856. It was a tit-for-tat affair between abolitionist John Brown and his followers, and Capt. Henry Pate and his men. Pate and his troops were duty-bound to round up Brown and his boys for killing five pro-slavers at nearby Pottawatomie Creek.

In retaliation Pate captured three of Brown's men near Palmyra, now Baldwin City. Pate continued to search for Brown and found him. Trouble was that 28 of Pate's men ended up captured by Brown. A historical marker in Robert Hall Pearson Park on U.S. 56 tells of the various encounters between Brown and Pate.

Now, about this Maple Leaf Festival.

Seems these folks have a bunch of beautiful maple trees lining the streets of Baldwin City, and that's about all the excuse they need to have a party. I took a peek at the invitation, and you're all invited.

The festival started in 1957 and has expanded to include an arts and crafts fair on the downtown streets, a parade on Saturday, country and western and

The Baldwin City Depot is home to the "Train to Nowhere," a popular ride which takes passengers south of Baldwin toward a point known as "Nowhere."

SANTA FE DEPOT 1906

NATIONAL REGISTER OF

HISTORIC PLACES 1983

bluegrass music, and a variety of displays at the junior high school.

At each festival the Rotarian Tourmasters load visitors into busses for a tour of the many historic sites in and around Baldwin City. Add to that the potential for a ride on the "Train to Nowhere" and you've got a pretty busy weekend if you choose to visit Baldwin City in October.

About that train to Nowhere: On Aug. 8, 1987, the Midland Historic Railroad began operating on its 11 miles of track between Baldwin City and a place called Nowhere, somewhere near Ottawa. The railroad operates from April through Oct. 29.

For more information on the annual Maple Leaf Festival and the train, call the city clerk at (785) 594-6427.

Baldwin City came about in 1857 when John Baldwin arrived from Ohio and built a saw and gristmill at Fifth and Indiana streets. His other interest, besides business, was to build a better society through Christian education.

The Methodists thought Baldwin had a pretty good idea and founded Baker University there in 1858. It is the oldest four-year college in Kansas. When you visit Baker University be sure to find the Old Castle Museum Complex, the Rev. Thomas Coole Chinese Coin Collection and the Bishop William A. Quayle Rare Bible Collection. The Bible collection includes clay

cuneiform tablets from the time of Abraham, some Gutenberg stuff and a whole bunch of rare and unique Bibles, English and American.

The brick streets of Baldwin City are said to have been laid by one man — an Oneida Indian named Jim Garfield Brown. He began paving on Dec. 8, 1925, and finished the job on Aug. 15, 1926. Brown was so fast that he could lay bricks quicker than they could be brought to him.

From Baldwin City take the county road north to the Douglas State Fishing Lake. Although the lake level varies some from year to year you'll find good camping and fishing in a mighty pretty place.

From Baldwin, as it is generally known, we'll travel north for a visit to Vinland. Originally known as Coal Creek, the small village eventually took its name from the surrounding vineyards owned by a fellow named Barnes.

The Coal Creek Library was established there in 1859 as the Coal Creek Social Library. It was originally a subscription library, one that required dues of 50 cents per year. Members would sing, have readings and play parlor games at biweekly meetings. It's Kansas' oldest library in continuous use, and is open each Sunday from the first Sunday in April through early November from noon to 4 p.m.

To arrange for a visit on another day, call librarian Martha Smith at (785) 594-3960.

The airport at Vinland houses quite a few aircraft for such a small community. A number of pilots from Baldwin City, Lawrence and Kansas City hangar their aircraft alongside the grass runway. A plaque on the northeast corner of the airfield is dedicated to Delbert William Chaney. Chaney created the Vinland Valley Aerodrome on July 25, 1969, and was killed in 1975 when his crop duster crashed north of Vinland. The privately owned airport has public gas and maintenance facilities. Drop in, flaps down, for a visit.

From Vinland drive north for about five miles, then left (west) for two miles to Wells Overlook Park. The park is on the highest point, 1,600 feet, in the Wakarusa Valley. Wakarusa, by the way, is the name of the river that defined this beautiful valley and continues to help feed Clinton Reservoir. Depending on who you talk to, Wakarusa means "River of Big Weeds" or "Hip Deep."

Climb to the top of the observation tower for a 360-degree view which takes in most of Douglas County. Land for the park was donated by William Wells in 1971. The park has excellent playground facilities, several hiking trails and a sheltered picnic area for larger groups.

Eudora, about 11 miles northeast, was founded in 1857 by German settlers and named for Eudora Fish. Her father, a Shawnee Indian named Paschal Fish Jr., built a log cabin called the Fish House on the Freemont-Westport Trail in 1854. The two-room cabin served as a way station for stagecoach passengers and for covered wagons as they traveled west.

There are more than ninety 100-year-old homes in Eudora. Two buildings you should visit are the Holy Family Catholic Church at 9th and Church and the Eudora School at 731 Maple. The church was built in 1864, the school in 1860. Today the school, which also served as city hall, is a private home.

Lawrence, the peaceful hilltop home of the University of Kansas and Mount Oread, holds a grisly place in Civil War history. The town, platted in 1855, was named for Amos A. Lawrence, a wealthy manufacturer and treasurer of the New England Immigrant Aid Company. Lawrence, who hailed from Massachusetts, is said to have deplored having a town named in his honor because it "would give the appearance of promoting my own celebrity."

The University of Kansas was established there in 1866 followed by Haskell Indian Institute, now Haskell Indian Junior College, in 1884. Lawrence is also the birthplace of basketball.

On Aug. 21, 1863, William Quantrill and his cowardly bunch of pro-slavery cutthroats entered Lawrence like a bad dream at 5 a.m. For the next four hours they killed, raped, looted and burned. When the raid ended, 150 citizens of Lawrence lay dead in the streets.

Quantrill had targeted Lawrence because it was viewed as a nest of free-staters. It was also home to James Lane, an infamous Jayhawker who conducted a similar raid against pro-slavers in Osceola, Mo., on Sept. 23, 1861.

To better understand the history of Douglas County, you should stop by the Watkins Community Museum at 1047 Massachusetts in Lawrence. The museum serves as the repository of Douglas County historical information. It's open Tuesday through Friday from 10 a.m. to 4 p.m. and Saturday and Sunday from 1 to 4 p.m. Admission is free.

The "Map of Historic Douglas County" is available at the museum. For my money, $7 to be exact, it is the finest county historical map that I've come across during my Kansas travels. The map has all of the county roads. It lists names and locates 137 historic buildings, tells when they were built and how they're currently used and includes photographs of 33 of them. If more counties had maps like this, Kansans would know a lot more about their state. To buy the map, call the museum at (785) 841-4109.

Another fascinating place to visit is the Museum of Natural History on the University of Kansas campus. Just a look at the stately limestone building, listed on the National Register of Historic Places, is worth the trip, but it's only the icing on the cake. Inside you'll find a marvelous collection of nearly one million fossils, amphibians, reptiles, birds and mammals from the Great Plains in 150 exhibits.

In addition to the static displays there are live bees doing their thing, fish swimming about and land snakes alive! And there's also Comanche, the only member of the 7th Cavalry who had the good sense to duck at the Battle of the Little Bighorn on June 25, 1876.

Comanche was the mount of Capt. Myles Keogh and was wounded several times during the battle. He died in 1891 at the age of 28 and is on permanent display at the museum.

Museum hours are 8 a.m. to 5 p.m. Monday through Saturday, 1 to 5 p.m. Sundays and holidays. Admission is free; however, donations are accepted. For more information, call (785) 864-4540 weekdays, (785) 864-4450 weekends.

There is much to see in Lawrence so take your time, visit the shops on Massachusetts Street and roam through the KU campus. An interesting thing about the north-south streets is that they are, for the most part, named after states according to when the states were admitted to the union.

Drive north from Lawrence and take the road paralleling the Kansas River to Bald Eagle or, as it is called now, Lecompton. Once a bastion of fervent pro-slavers, the Lecompton of today is a quiet, tree-shaded community. A large sign on the east entrance to town proclaims its historic roots.

Downtown, on North Elmore Street, is Constitution Hall. Built in 1855 to house the Territorial Legislature, it was the site where the Lecompton Constitution was drafted in 1857. Through their proposed constitution the pro-slave legislators hoped to make Kansas a slave state. They failed and the free-staters moved the capital to Topeka while the pro-slavers remained in Lecompton. Built in 1892, the stone city jail with its original door and barred window, sits behind Constitution Hall.

Lecompton is also the home of Lane University, now known as the Lane University Museum. Built in 1882 and jointly operated by the United Brethren Church of Christ and Lane University, it closed in 1902. President Dwight Eisenhower's parents met while attending school there.

The Stull cemetery is our next stop. On a hill overlooking the cemetery are the ruins of the Evangelical Emmanuel Church. The limestone building was constructed in 1867, and church services were conducted in German up until 1908. It was originally called Deer Creek Church.

From Stull take County Road 1023 south to Clinton Reservoir and Clinton. The small pioneer community of Clinton sits on a peninsula leading to the lake and state park. Created in 1980, the reservoir is approximately 7,000 acres and was the first Kansas reservoir where bald eagles successfully produced young in modern times. The view to the east of the park is unusual in that Mount Oread and the University of Kansas campus appear to be on top of the dam. From there you can camp, picnic or sail while looking at KU. Unless, of course, you are a K-State grad or fan.

From there drive southeast on County Road 458 to Road 1029, where you turn south to Lone Star Lake. It's one of those small, gemstone lakes that Kansas has so many of, but Kansans know so little about. Created in the 1930s by the Civilian Conservation Corps, the 195-acre lake has a small resort community along part of its wooded shoreline. It's a public-use lake that's better seen than described, but in a word, it's idyllic. The lake takes its name from the nearby community.

History has it that settlers built a school in Lone Star but couldn't agree on a name. One sparkling night, following a school meeting, one of the settlers looked up into the twilight sky and pointed out a solitary star. Another person suggested the name, and there you have it. A school, a town and a lake — all named because of an unknown prairie romantic.

A Marion County farmer takes the time to wave to a motorist while cutting wheat.

Fort Riley: Protector of the Santa Fe and Oregon Trails

Fort Riley stands out as a rich blend of history, tradition

At one time or another every Kansan, native or naturalized, ought to spend a day at historic Fort Riley, located in Geary County. The beautifully maintained post is a stunning sight to see and offers plenty of opportunities for a close look at its rich history and traditions.

Located next to where the Smoky Hill and Republican rivers meet to form the Kansas River, Fort Riley was activated in 1852 as Camp Center (or Camp Centre), primarily because it was thought to be near the geographic center of the United States.

Its primary mission was to provide protection for settlers moving west along the Santa Fe, Oregon and Mormon trails. In June 1853 it was renamed Fort Riley, shortly after the death of Gen. Bennet Riley, a distinguished veteran of the Mexican War. He commanded the first military escort down the Santa Fe Trail in June 1829. Riley's troops escorted 60 men and 36 wagons to their destination and returned to Kansas in November 1829.

Since Fort Riley was the home of the U.S. Cavalry School and the cavalry branch of the service (until it ceased to exist in 1950), it was appropriate that it also become home to the U.S. Cavalry Museum in 1962.

The museum is a showcase for the history of the "horse soldiers" and their traditions. The museum, housed in the old post hospital, is one of the four original limestone buildings from the 1850s. It receives more than 70,000 tourists each year. In 1890 the hospital was turned into the post headquarters.

The museum displays feature a comprehensive look at cavalry history, including the famous 7th Cavalry, formed at Fort Riley in 1866. The famous Buffalo Soldiers, a black cavalry unit with white officers in the 9th and 10th U.S. Cavalry regiments, are also represented in the museum.

At any one time there are more than 1,800 of the 8,000 museum-owned artifacts on display. The historic displays, the life-like dioramas as well as two original works by Frederic Remington, combine to accurately depict frontier life for the troopers at Fort Riley.

The well-stocked gift shop on the first floor is full of items about Fort Riley and dozens of military books on a variety of related subjects. You can also pick up an information-packed Fort Riley Walking Tour booklet. The walk takes about 45 minutes and is a little more than one mile long.

What does it cost to visit this museum? Not a penny — but the museum isn't against accepting donations. If you have any questions, just ask any of the museum staffers. And don't forget to ask about the ghosts at Fort Riley, in particular the ghost of Quarters 24.

Which brings us to Custer House, a very short walk from the museum. Turns out that old George and his missus didn't really live in Quarters 24. A bookkeeping glitch had them in #24 when in fact they lived in #21, just down the street. In any case the Custers lived at Fort Riley in 1866.

Built for $3,500 in 1855, Custer House is the only double set of officers' quarters left standing from that era. Made of smooth native limestone, this simple but elegant example of frontier military housing is open to visitors, free of charge, with tours being conducted by volunteer members of the Fort Riley Historical Society

Just a stone's throw from Custer House is the Old Trooper Monument. Patterned after a drawing by Frederic Remington and nicknamed "Old Bill," this monument is also the grave site of Chief, the last cavalry horse on government payrolls. Chief was retired in 1950 and died in 1968. He was buried standing upright at the base of the monument. Ain't tradition grand?

Behind Old Trooper is a parade field, often used for Change of Command ceremonies. If there is one place you will still see mounted troopers at Fort Riley it will be on that parade ground. The special mounted unit at Fort Riley uses the field to practice in preparation for various military and civilian displays.

Since you're at the corner of Forsyth and Sheridan, you might as well drive north on Forsyth to Barry. On both sides and directly in front of you will be the quarters of the highest-ranking officers at Fort Riley. Generals Hap Arnold and Jonathan Wainwright once lived on Forsyth. The quarters are some of the most attractive and well-kept limestone homes in Kansas.

Turn left on Barry and visit St. Mary's Chapel, the oldest stone church in Kansas. Built in 1855, it is one of the four remaining buildings from that period.

All of these places are within walking distance of Custer House.

After your walking tour you might want to take a short drive to visit the bison at the Buffalo Corral. Just before the corral, tucked into a beautifully maintained area, is a military cemetery. From there you might want to have a picnic lunch at either of the post's two youngster-oriented parks. Both Wyman and McCormick parks offer picnic tables, grills and playground equipment.

Speaking of the outdoors, it's important to note that Fort Riley has the second-largest continuous public hunting and fishing area in Kansas, covering more than 69,000 acres of prairie with eight lakes and ponds stocked with channel and flathead catfish, bass, bluegill, northern pike, crappie, flathead catfish, green sunfish and trout.

Fort Riley hunting and fishing permits are required and can be obtained at the Outdoor Recreation Center. Check with post information to find the ORC building.

As long as you're on the east end of Huebner Road, you definitely need to stop in at Kansas' First Territorial Capitol Museum. Built of native limestone, this impressive two-story, 40-by-80 foot structure housed the first meeting of the Kansas Territorial Legislature in the summer of 1855.

Legislators arrived June 30 to find a building with no roof or floor. They worked day and night for two days finishing the floor and roof but still had no doors. Open door meetings took on a historic meaning during those first sessions of the Kansas Legislature.

Just outside and behind the First Territorial Capitol is a wonderful natural experience. The Kaw River Nature Trails take you through a riparian wonderland filled with sights and sounds unique to the Kansas River floodplain. A booklet available at the Territorial Capitol is filled with information about the history of the river. It also has descriptions and drawings of plants and animals, making it a very helpful companion on the self-guided tour.

As you walk down the 24 steps from the top of the trailhead you become immersed in a natural wonderland beneath the lush green canopy of mas-

An elk hunter surveys the grasslands of the 80,000-acre public hunting area on Fort Riley. The Fort Riley elk herd produces some of the largest trophy elk in Kansas.

sive hardwoods and cottonwoods.
Signs along the trail identify the various species of trees and plants. The
area feels much like the jungle where
the only sounds are your footfalls and
the birds singing from the treetops.
Light occasionally pierces the canopy,
dancing on the forest floor or streaking
across the side of an ivy-laden cottonwood.

When you arrive at the Kansas River
you must choose to hike right or left.
You win in either case as you experience the flora and fauna that form,
grow and live in and along the river's
edge. If you're lucky you will see a pair
of nesting wood ducks but they spook
easily, so move quietly.

For more information: U.S. Cavalry
Museum, (785) 239-2737. First
Territorial Capitol, (785) 784-5535.

A monument to "Old Trooper" is the center-piece of one of the parade grounds on Fort Riley. Buried, standing up, in front of the monument is "Chief," the last horse on the U.S. Government rolls. The monument is located across the street from Custer House, a popu-lar tourist attraction.

A journey back to days of cannoneers, dragoons

Military history on the frontier comes alive at Fort Scott

The year, 1847. The place, Buena Vista, Mexico.

Dragoons and infantry of Company A, Fort Scott, Kan., under the command of Gen. Zachary Taylor, wait for Gen. Santa Anna's numerically superior troops to attack.

The gunner estimates Mexican troops to be 800 to 1,000 yards from his gun crew's front. Sharply, he turns and barks out the command, "Action front. Shell, two seconds!"

Cannoneers manning the six-pound field artillery piece react to his command, knowing that their speed and accuracy may determine the outcome of the battle. Working methodically, they load, sponge and ram the explosive charge into the barrel. Tapping the left side of the artillery piece, the gunner indicates the direction of fire.

Number 3 cannoneer immediately responds by adjusting the spike to the gunner's new direction of fire.

"Ready!"

Number 4 cannoneer steps away from the piece, pivots to receive the already burning port-fire staff, and awaits the command. Santa Anna's troops start their assault. The battle has begun.

"Fire!" commands the gunner as the port-fire staff begins its arc to the primer. As the fire touches powder, the fuse blossoms to life...sssssssss — kaBOOOOM!!! The 6-pounder sallies

forth its thunderous response to the Mexicans' advance. It is the first of many volleys that will eventually spell defeat for Santa Anna's army in its war against the United States.

It's in the history books now, but the event did happen.

Dragoons were an elite combination of cavalry and infantry. And the Dragoons from Fort Scott were to become a decisive factor in the United States' defeat of Santa Anna's men during the Battle of Buena Vista.

To get from Wichita to Fort Scott in Bourbon County is mighty easy — just take U.S. 54 all the way to Fort Scott.

The Fort Scott National Historic Site of today, completely restored and operated by the National Park Service, sits on its original location next to downtown Fort Scott. The journey there is well worth the drive — particularly if you enjoy a living history lesson given by volunteer men and women who dress in period costumes and relive the daily rigors of Army life in 1845.

On the parade field you'll see soldiers marching to the cadence call. A dragoon sergeant serves his duty at the guardhouse in full-dress uniform, uniquely styled apparel based on those worn by Napoleon's officers. The dragoons were some of the most impressive-looking military figures of their day.

In the shade of the enlisted men's barracks, a laundress peels and dices turnips for an evening meal. Several times each day, bugle calls echo across the immaculate parade grounds, calling the troops to reveille, stable duty, mess and, at day's end, taps.

All these scenarios and characters are on stage for one reason — to make the history, events and lifestyle of 1845 come alive. Fort Scott is no museum with all its exhibits behind glass. Full-time park service rangers, part-time summer help and hundreds of volunteers make up a cast dedicated to entertaining and educating visitors.

Each of the volunteers has a personal interest in pre-Civil War history. These folks aren't the automaton-like tour guides found in amusement parks; they're serious history buffs with a penchant for detail.

"It's the only Mexican War era fort in the national park system," said Stephen Miller, former park superintendent. "There's a rich undiscovered history in eastern Kansas. The more we learn through historical documentation, the more we realize the high level of activity there was in this area."

Miller said that the 1st and 2nd Kansas Colored Volunteer Infantry regiments were mustered at Fort Scott in 1863. They were the first all-black regiments mustered from a Union state. The 1st was mustered into service before the 54th regiment of Massachusetts, the unit featured in

"Glory," a film depicting a black Civil War regiment.

The National Park Service acquired the site in 1979 and spent much of the next three years resurrecting the old fort from its foundations. Restoration of the three existing officers' quarters and the reconstruction of the other buildings were accomplished by using original drawings and photographs for reference.

The visitors center has Park Service personnel to answer questions and an outstanding slide show that relates the complete history of the fort and the campaigns its troops participated in, and depicts daily barracks life and the tedium of existence at a western outpost of the 1840s.

In addition to the visitors center, there are a museum and bookstore, dragoon and infantry barracks, dragoon stables (horses got better treatment than the troops, the philosophy being that a man without a horse is just an infantryman), officers' quarters (original buildings), a blacksmith shop, a bakery (used during special-event weekends to supply bread to the mess hall), a powder magazine, and a fairly uncomfortable guardhouse for those who wouldn't toe the mark.

The historic site has 20 historic structures, of which 11 are original. Nine were reconstructed. Within the restored buildings are 33 historically restored

Dragoon reenactors at Fort Scott show several youngsters how to load, clean and fire the 6-pound cannon at the eastern edge of the grounds. Each Sunday the Dragoons (a combination of cavalry and foot soldiers) demonstrate firing procedures and then fire both the 5- and 12-pound cannons.

Fort Scott National Cemetery #1. Established during President Lincoln's tenure in office, Fort Scott was the first name selected when numbering the national cemeteries. The picturesque cemetery is the final resting place for soldiers (Union and Confederate) and Indian scouts from the Civil War through Desert Storm.

rooms. Self-guided tours pamphlets are available at the visitor's center.

One of the weekend highlights is a demonstration of two field artillery pieces at 2 p.m. Sundays. One of the park rangers plays the part of a dragoon sergeant and explains firing procedures, types of projectiles and their application in a battlefield situation.

After the sergeant's lecture, the gun crew goes through a dry fire of the cannon. Then it's "boom time" — time to fire both the 6-pounder and the 12-pound mountain howitzer. Once the dust settles, visitors are invited to ask questions and take a closer look at both guns.

Weekends are the best time to visit because both days are filled with drills, guided tours, weapons firing, interpretative programs (call ahead for program details) and a retreat ceremony.

On the second weekend in April each year some 125 to 150 volunteers gather for the Civil War Encampment. Although there were no Civil War battles fought by soldiers from Fort Scott, the garrison was manned by Union soldiers during the conflict.

The biggest weekend of the year, however, is the Mexican War Encampment on the first weekend after Labor Day. Twenty-five to 30 mounted dragoons and as many infantrymen plus laundresses and officers and their wives will play it to the hilt for two action-packed days with demonstrations of horse skills, lance and saber drills, artillery demonstrations, inspections, mess duty and a special interpretative program Saturday evening.

The second weekend in October is the American Indian Heritage Weekend and Mountain Man Rendezvous, popular events with Indian dancing and other cultural and educational programs on the Osage Indian. The Rendezvous provides a look at traditional lodges and lifestyles of fur trappers and traders in the 1840s.

In early December Fort Scott opens its doors during the evening for the Frontier Candlelight Tours. The 54 tours (18 per night), take place over a three-day weekend in December and are by reservation only. The tours are so popular that all reservations are filled on Nov. 1, the first day reservations are taken. More than 1,100 people take the Candlelight Frontier Tours each year.

"This site (Fort Scott) tends to lend itself to the living-history concept very well because we have a completely restored site," said one former park superintendent. "It brings to life that (1840s) historic period, and the public particularly enjoys that."

Admission is $1 for everyone 17 to 61 years old. The fort is open daily from 8:30 a.m. to 5 p.m. Call (316) 223-0310 for information on weekend thematic programs at Fort Scott National Historic Site.

The Fort Scott Tourist Information Center in the Chamber of Commerce office can be reached seven days a week at (800) 245-3678. Folks at the center will send you information packets on events and sites in Fort Scott, including the Historic Homes Tour, Trolley Tour of Fort Scott, Living History Walking Tour and the Ralph Richardson Museum, featuring a restored Victorian apartment upstairs.

Another Fort Scott attraction is National Cemetery No. 1, one of the 12 original national cemeteries. It's located at the end of National Street in the southeast part of Fort Scott.

The small but beautifully maintained cemetery is the final resting ground for soldiers from the Indian Wars through Vietnam. Also interred there are the remains of 16 Indian soldiers, all buried within a 35-day period at the end of 1862. Was there a battle? No one seems to know.

The Indian graves are situated at the north side of the cemetery toward the entrance. Look for grave marker #8 — "Stick Out Belly" or #22 "Deer-In-Water". The cemetery also holds the graves of 13 Confederate soldiers who died while imprisoned at Fort Scott. Their markers are easy to find as they're set at an angle, not in line with the markers of the Union Soldiers.

The most unusual marker is that of Eugene F. Ware, interred in grave #1. During the Civil War, Ware served the Union as a captain in the 7th Iowa Cavalry. During his years in Kansas he wrote a great number of poems, most notably "Ironquill" and "John Brown". The site of Ware's grave, as well as that of his wife, is marked with a large, native sandstone boulder.

If you enjoy Fort Scott, why not try some of Kansas' other forts? Here's a listing of phone numbers to call for more information.

Other Forts in Kansas:
Fort Leavenworth - (785) 684-5604
Fort Riley - (785) 239-2737
Fort Larned - (316) 285-6911
Fort Hays - (785) 625-6812
Fort Dodge - (316) 227-2121
Fort Harker - (785) 472-4071
Fort Wallace - (785) 891-3538

Did You Know?

Name the counties in the four corners of Kansas.
Cheyenne (northwest), Morton (southwest), Doniphan (northeast) and Cherokee (southeast)

Who raised the first American flag in Kansas in 1806?
Zebulon Pike

Who was the first governor elected in Kansas who was born in Kansas?
Arthur Capper, 1915-19

Where was Amelia Earhart's home?
Atchison in Atchison County

Where was Emmett Kelly from?
Sedan in Chautauqua County

Where was the first baseball game played under lights?
Independence in Montgomery County

A Fort Scott dragoon, with his clay pipe and musket, stands 'at ease' next to his tent.

What Kansan discovered Pluto?
Clyde Tombaugh of Burdett in Pawnee County. In high school Tombaugh was nicknamed "Comet Clyde". A small plaque honoring him is near the Burdett water tower.

William Allen White and what noted scientist received honorary degrees at Harvard in 1935?
Albert Einstein

Why were oxen preferable to horses to pull freight over the Santa Fe Trail?
Oxen were steadier and the Indians didn't want them.

Who was the first woman elected to represent Kansas as a member of the U.S. Congress?
Kathryn O'Loughlin, 1932-34, Democrat

Who was the silent-film comedian born at Piqua in 1896?
Buster Keaton

What is the name of the tall grass the Flint Hills are famous for?
Big Bluestem

In the state Capitol mural, what is John Brown holding in his left hand?
The Bible

What Kansan of Indian descent was the first woman permitted to plead before the U.S. Supreme Court?
Lydia B. Conley

What Kansan was the first woman in the world who was fully trained in dentistry?
Lucy Hobbs Taylor

The flags of what six nations have flown over what is now Kansas?
Great Britain, France, Spain, Mexico, United States and Texas

When the five Plains tribes were forced to cede land to Kansas settlers, to what state were they removed?
Oklahoma

Where did George "Honey Boy" Evans, who wrote the words to "In the Good Old Summer Time", spend his youth?
Kinsley in Edwards County

What year and where did the Republican Party organize in Kansas?
1859 in Osawatomie in Miami County

What year was the meadowlark chosen as the state bird?
1925

The only exclusively Indian burying ground in the United States is in Kansas. Name it.
Huron Cemetery in Wyandotte County

Kingman County and 'The Queen of the Ninnescah'

Kingman's varied landscape and rich history offer travelers a full day of memorable experiences

How many Kansas counties have a county seat with the same name as the county? You'll get the answer at the end of this day trip to Kingman County, which, by the way, is one of those counties.

Located about 40 miles west of Wichita, Kingman County is a place you should visit. Shaped much like Kansas with Cheney Reservoir notching the northeast corner, this bountiful county will fill your day with a variety of interesting experiences.

According to the Kansas Geological Survey, Kingman County is comprised of three physiographic regions: a good dose of the High Plains, a healthy amount of Wellington Lowlands all accented with an introduction to the Gypsum Hills. This information makes a lot more sense however, if you have the new Kansas highway map provided by the Kansas Department of Transportation and Planning. The maps are free.

The state map highlights physiographic provinces of Kansas, which allows you to know at a glance the manner of geology you are traveling through. It's color-coded, easy to read and has an index of the provinces on the left side of the map. Using it as you travel throughout the state should contribute to a better understanding of Kansas geology.

But I digress.

I don't know about everyone else, but I love rivers and streams. Lakes are wonderful in their own way but lack the charm of a living, meandering waterway, something that has carved its own path through Kansas.

The Ninnescah River is one of my favorite ribbons of water, and Kingman County is one of the few places where the public has a fair amount of access to this sand-bottomed, clear-water river. It is unfortunate that only one percent of Kansas is available for public recreational use, so when you have a chance to visit a river without having to ask permission, you ought to take that opportunity.

The best and most scenic access to the Ninnescah is the 4,000-acre Byron Walker Wildlife Area, seven miles west of Kingman on U.S. 54. You can pick up a map of the area at the area's headquarters, adjacent to U.S. 54, right before the road south to Zenda. If you aren't paying attention, you'll miss the turn south into the Wildlife Area's office.

Within the wildlife area are several access points to the river, but my favorite is the road south off U.S. 54 into the wildlife area and just west of the road north to Penalosa.

This sandy road will accommodate most vehicles, so go ahead, make your day and drive on down to the river. When you get to a fork in the road you can either turn right and drive a short distance to a small but deep fishing pond. Or, you can turn left and drive to an oxbow in the river where you can picnic, hike or fish. This is a wildlife area, so take the normal precautions and bring insect repellent.

There are no picnic tables, fireplaces or rest rooms by the river, but what the heck, this is an adventure!

All of the roads within the wildlife area are lined with native grasses, sand plum thickets and the wildlife who make their home in this balanced natural environment. I had the good fortune to receive a guided tour of the area by its namesake, Byron Walker, the Johnny Appleseed of Kingman County. Walker was the man responsible for managing this area for 41 years until his retirement in 1988 from what was then called the Kansas Fish and Game Department.

Walker, a self-taught naturalist, spent his working life restoring this cattle-ravaged landscape to a lush sand hill prairie environment. Many of the trees and shrubs were hand-planted by Walker, including all of the big trees lining the eastern shore of Kingman State Fishing Lake.

The 144-acre spring-fed lake is a fine place to spend the day fishing, hiking the nature trails, bird watching or just relaxing under the cottonwood canopy as the leaves shimmer and dance on a summer breeze. If you only have time to visit one place in Kingman County, the Byron Walker Wildlife Area will do quite nicely.

Assuming, however, that you have the

The old Cunningham city jail (l) and train depot are now tourist attractions in Cunningham, a Kingman County community on U.S. 54.

day to travel, I would start in Kingman. Originally called Sherman in 1872, it was renamed Kingman two years later in honor of Samuel Kingman, chief justice of the Kansas Supreme Court.

As folks settled into the area, things were pretty busy at Kingman in the late 1800s. Pure rock salt was discovered in 1887. Several industries — including broom and fire extinguisher factories, an iron foundry, planing mill, gristmill and two water-driven flour mills — provided the town's economic base.

Kingman also had four newspapers, which, I suspect, provided more news than readers could possibly use. But this was frontier time and when a

town calls itself the "Queen of the Ninnescah" it had better look busy.

The Kingman of today continues to be a busy town. As you drive down the main street you'll be rolling over bricks that were made in Cleveland, a town once located five miles south of Kingman. If you're interested in a closer look at the county's past you should visit the Kingman County Historical Museum, housed in a more than 100-year-old building that has also served as the city building and fire house.

It's a large, red brick structure with twin spires. According to Walker, former president of the Kingman County Historical Society, it's the only remaining firehouse in Kansas with a hose-drying tower. The museum is open Fridays from 9 a.m. to 4 p.m. or by calling (316) 532-2627.

Driving east from Kingman you should stop at Waterloo, a small white church with a spire pinpoints its location to the north of U.S. 54, just as you pass over Smoots Creek. The reason for the stop is to visit Kansas' oldest arboretum, a small grove of trees just north of the baseball diamond. The grove was planted by nurseryman John Riggs in 1885. It includes a wide variety of trees from foreign lands. Take your tree identification book and see if you can pick out the royal English oak or alligator cedar.

Five miles south of Waterloo is Murdock, named in honor of Col. Marsh Murdock, founder of The Wichita Eagle. Originally called New Murdock in 1884, it was renamed Murdock in 1918 after a town by the same name in Butler County closed its post office and then faded into obscurity.

From Murdock take the road south for three miles, east for five miles, then south to Norwich. Norwich is a good place to stop for lunch and look around. On the drive there you'll cross the Ninnescah three times as it winds south through the county. Drive slowly and keep your camera at the ready. There are lots of wildlife along the river and they won't wait for you to get your camera out of the bag, take off the "never-ready case" and remove the lens cap.

About seven miles west of Norwich on K-42 is Adams. Stop at the high school on the north side of the road and try the old swings and teeter-totters in the school yard.

Four miles north is Belmont. Things are pretty slow in Belmont these days, but the town does have a footnote in the aviation history books. Clyde Cessna grew up a few miles to the south. It was there that he built and piloted his first plane, patterned on a French monoplane, in 1911. His nephew, Dwane Wallace, grew up in Belmont and went on to work with his uncle to develop and produce Cessna aircraft in Wichita.

Back on K-42 and another five or so miles west is Rago where, in the late 1980s, the local folks were embroiled in a dispute with the U.S. Postal Service. The service wanted to close the town's small but interesting post office. If you get there between 8 and 10 a.m. you can visit with folks and get the lowdown for yourself. If it's closed you know the Postal Service has won the dispute and rural America has lost another piece of its past.

Right next to the post office is a bold but rusty sign announcing the location of the ballpark. A short drive reveals a "Field of Dreams" gone weedy. I suspect this was once a busy place, but time has left only memories and some pretty interesting photographic opportunities if you're there early or late in the day.

My most vivid memory of Rago, named for the Rago Trading Post once located southeast of town, is being on a roofing crew that in the early 1960s slathered a very slippery, silvery roofing material onto the top of the bins at the grain elevator. If you'll notice there are no railings around the bins. One slip and we could have easily become a story still told in Rago.

About five miles west of Rago is Spivey, named for Rueben M. Spivey, president of the Arkansas Valley Town and Land Company. This small but ambitious town has its city limit sign posted an economically aggressive half-mile from town. The relatively new post office building and several small but thriving businesses show that Spivey means to grow rather than fade into history.

An interesting bit of history occurred in Spivey in the late 1800s when local ranchers told area settlers of an imminent raid by Indians. The settlers rounded up their families, hustled into Spivey then holed up in a red brick building that still stands.

As the evening wore on and no Indian war party showed up, the settlers decided to have their own party and danced into the early morning hours. It was later discovered that the ranchers were just trying to spook the settlers into leaving. Guess it didn't work. As an aside, the first girl born in Spivey was named Spivey Belle Treadway.

Farther west on K-42 is Zenda. First known as Rochester and then replatted as New Rochester, it was finally changed to Zenda to avoid any confusion caused by the two names. The folks at the community building probably can explain those transitions a lot better than I can — and while you're there, take a look at the five-panel historic mural on the north side of the building.

Six miles north of Zenda is the squeaky-clean town of Willowdale. Originally named Peters in 1884, the small community was the creation of Francis Weinschenk, an Iowa farmer in search of a good place to raise crops and a large family.

His son Tony opened a small store in the family home. In no time at all several more families moved into the area. As the town was settled they decided to call it Peters, with Tony being appointed as the first postmaster. The town's name was changed to Willowdale in 1900.

Sitting atop this hillside town is St. Peter's Catholic Church. Built in 1882, it stands gleaming white against a powder-blue sky. The Willowdale folks think a lot of the church. Their pride shows through its upkeep and the immaculate grounds surrounding the church and adjacent buildings.

A surprise awaits as you travel west out of town. A quick glance to the north reveals a "Peacock Crossing" sign followed by another sign proclaiming the "Roadside Inn."

What inn? All I could see was a farmhouse with two signs.

Looking closer, I drove in the U-shaped driveway and around back sat a tavern. Now, this is no ordinary place, I said to myself. Fortunately, I arrived at 4 p.m., just in time for owner Louella Schmitz to open up for the day.

With a smile that would light every corner of a dark room, Schmitz proudly said that her pub had been in business in Willowdale for the past 60 years. Originally called the Chicken House, it was renamed the Roadside Inn in 1962. "Everyone says this place is unique," said Schmitz. One customer told her, "It was just like going to Colorado — just add the mountains."

Schmitz and her mother, Josephine, run the inn and limit their business to beer and snacks. A jukebox provides the music and the patrons add the atmosphere to round out this colorful Kingman County tavern.

Another interesting aspect of Willowdale is the wetland along the east edge of town. The spring-fed marsh is surrounded by cypress trees, the bulbous tentacles at the base of each tree reaching into the luscious, clear water filled with large bluegill and other panfish.

To round out your county tour you can meander southwest from Willowdale to Nashville, a town said to have been named "Old Bross" before it was moved next to the railroad and renamed in honor of Gen. Francis Nash, a North Carolinian killed by a cannonball during a Revolutionary War battle in 1777.

From Nashville travel north to St. Leo, named for one of the 21 saints named Leo. From St. Leo continue north to Cunningham on U.S. 54. Cunningham came into being after the nearby town of Ninnescah was destroyed by a tornado. James Cunningham offered two lots to anyone who would settle in the town that he platted in the shape of a cross. Check it out from the air.

From Cunningham drive north to Penalosa, the only town in Kansas named for a governor of New Mexico, specifically Don Diego Dionisio de Penalosa Briceno y Berdugo. Certainly a lot jazzier name than Penalosa's original name... Lotta.

Each Kingman County town or ghost town has a unique history. The local folks, if they have some history in the area, will be more than willing to help you explore their town's past.

P.S. — The number of counties in Kansas with the same name for their county seat is 14.

In the Kansas center of Swedish culture, with a touch of Scotland to boot

The old general would be proud of McPherson County today

I doubt that Gen. James Birdseye McPherson ever imagined that a county and county seat would be named in his honor. But if he were to visit today, he would be proud of his namesake in the heart of Kansas.

McPherson was killed in action during the battle of Atlanta on July 22, 1864. An impressive bronze statue of the West Point graduate stands surrounded by a lovely park, behind the beautifully renovated McPherson County Courthouse.

Driving to the McPherson County line is easy. From Wichita take I-135 north. When you get to Milepost 43, you're there.

While you're driving up the interstate, keep in mind that you're passing over the Equus Beds, the principal source of drinking water for Newton, McPherson and Wichita. The beds were named for the fossilized remains of Ice Age horses found in the sand, silt and gravel deposits throughout the area.

At Milepost 48, you'll pass over Black Kettle Creek, named for the Cheyenne chief killed by Gen. George Armstrong Custer's troops in Oklahoma. On your left will be Moundridge, home of the Wildcats, the 2A powerhouse tradition in girls and boys basketball. The town was named for a ridge running through Mound township.

Since you're in no hurry, I'd suggest you take the time to drive the streets of Moundridge, which is, according to its sign, "A Nice Place to Live." I'd have to agree.

About 12 miles on down the road is the McPherson exit. At Milepost 67 on your drive to McPherson, you'll be near the division between the McPherson Valley Lowlands and the Smoky Hills. Rivers and streams to the north drain into the Smoky Hill and Kansas rivers which eventually flow into the Missouri River. Rivers and creeks to the south drain into the Little Arkansas and Arkansas rivers, which end up in the Mississippi River.

The Smoky Hill River is the most meandering of all Kansas rivers. Folks who study the meanderings of rivers have found that in the 65 miles between the McPherson-Saline county line and Junction City, the Smoky Hill River twists and turns to the tune of 150 miles.

A sailboarder tries to catch the wind at McPherson State Fishing Lake while a couple fishes from one of the several jetties that jut out from the shoreline.

A visitor to Coronado Heights, located north of Lindsborg, takes a picture of two fellow travelers on a bus tour of north central Kansas.

won't find many trophy fish here, but the abundance of panfish makes it a great spot to get youngsters interested in fishing. The camping area is shaded by locust and Osage orange groves.

At the refuge manager's house on the east side of the area, are the remaining four trees of a large persimmon grove. Approximately 50 feet tall, the giant trees "had to be thick as dogs' hair and reaching for the sky to get that tall," said refuge manager Cliff Peterson.

At the southeast corner of the refuge is the Don Brown Memorial Gun Safety Range. The 100-yard public shooting range is open year-round to paper-target and clay-pigeon shooters. South of the refuge on County Road 304 is Canton, one of those nice towns with broad streets and a hot and cold water tower to give it some humor.

Canton, an Oriental name meaning "the wide east," was originally called Ostrog, a Polish name, but was later renamed after Canton, Ohio. It is also home to the McPherson County Fair and Kansas' only Lunker Bullhead Classic held every April to raise money for the Juvenile Diabetes Association.

To the west on U.S. 56 is Galva, a Swedish community named after Galva, Ill., and home to some of the shortest street signs I've seen. On the side of a downtown building the Galvanians have painted a nice thank-you card to World War II veterans.

In southwest McPherson County is Inman, named for Col. Henry Inman who once rode with Gen. Custer and became quartermaster general at Fort Harker, a frontier post that grew into the village of Kanopolis. Inman wrote several books about the West, many of them centering on Kansas and the Santa Fe Trail.

Inman, originally called Aiken, is a tightly woven Mennonite community that has some annual events you might want to put on your calendar. On the Fourth of July there is a large celebration and fireworks display at the Inman City Pasture on the northeast edge of town. And each October Inman puts on a two-day affair called the Town and Country Festival. Saturday is the big day with a parade, craft show and a community talent show.

At Christmas the town lights itself up with a large luminaria display that runs for five blocks, ending up in the Inman City Park where a live nativity scene is set up. The rest of the towns-folk jump into the Christmas spirit by putting up personal luminaria displays at their homes.

About 2 1/2 miles northeast of Inman is Lake Inman, the only remaining natural lake in Kansas. It was once part of what was called Chain of Lakes, a line of natural wetlands that ran from just west of McPherson south to the Harvey County line.

A herd of elk ventures out onto open ground at the McPherson Game Refuge. The photo was taken from the 25-foot high viewing platform located on the refuge.

History has it that a man named Schraug brought in a steam shovel in the early 1900s and drained the lakes so the land could be used for agriculture. Inman Lake was the only survivor of Schraug's steam shovel effort to convert natural wetlands to farmland.

The Kansas Department of Wildlife and Parks is in the process of buying land from willing sellers and has restored portions of the original wetlands to their natural state. The new area is called the McPherson Valley Wetlands, and is considered by upland game and waterfowl hunters as one of the hot spots for hunting in south-central Kansas.

The secrets of southwest Kansas

You'll find 108,000 acres of grasslands and plenty of room to roam in Morton County

Two busloads of youngsters from Ulysses, just up the road in Grant County, were champing at the bit to be just 20 feet south of where they stood. They fidgeted and listened while a representative of the U.S. Forest Service told them about the Santa Fe Trail and the history of Morton County.

But what they wanted to do most was run to the edge of Point of Rocks and scare themselves and their counselors silly. They wanted to lean into the wind and take a long look at the valley of the Cimarron River below.

History isn't always the most exciting thing for young people. But because it was presented by knowledgeable folks at the place where it happened, you can bet your bottom dollar that the youngsters from Ulysses had a thing or two to tell their parents when they got home that evening.

And so it goes in Morton County, one of the best-kept secrets in Kansas. When travelers drive through the southwest corner of Kansas, they generally don't have a clue about what they've just passed.

They fail to see the sweeping beauty of the Cimarron National Grasslands. And they probably don't know that the 108,000 acres that make up the grasslands constitute the largest area of public land in Kansas. The second largest is Fort Riley, and not all of its 80,000-plus acres are open to the public.

Knowing the locations of public land in Kansas is a good thing, especially when you consider that Kansas has the least amount of public land, only one percent, in the United States.

Travelers who fail to stop when rolling through Morton County toward Oklahoma and New Mexico will also miss the free history lesson readily available at the Morton County Historical Society Museum next to U.S. 56 at Elkhart.

The folks in Morton County take their history seriously. In 1986 one of the things they did to help celebrate the 100th anniversary of their county was to produce an 800-page book detailing the history of a place they call "The Cornerstone of Kansas."

To get to Morton County from Wichita I suggest you travel along U.S. 54 until one mile before Plains, a small town about 12 miles west of Meade. Don't forget to stop at the Meade County Historical Society Museum on U.S. 54 or the Dalton Gang Hideout at 502 S. Pearlette; both are in Meade, the Meade County seat.

Just before Plains, named for the landscape on which it stands, take the blacktop straight west to where it connects with U.S. 83/160. Turn south to K-51, then west again to Hugoton, the Stevens County seat.

Originally named Hugo in 1885 to honor the French writer Victor Hugo, it was later changed to Hugoton to avoid any possible postal confusion with Hugo, Colo. Natural gas was discovered near Hugoton in 1926. The Hugoton Gas Field continues to be one of the largest producers of natural gas in the United States. Be sure to visit the Stevens County Gas and Historical Museum while you're in Hugoton, "Home of the Eagles."

Several years ago when The Wichita Eagle was undergoing an external face-lift we had a contest to see who would get the large eagle adorning the top of our building. Hugoton High School was my choice, but the Boy Scouts of America won out. The eagle now proudly stands at the gateway to Camp Ta-Wa-Ko-Ni near Augusta.

From Hugoton take U.S. 56 to Feterita, named for a locally grown sorghum crop, and then on to Rolla, our first stop in Morton County.

According to John Rydjord, dean emeritus at Wichita State University and the author of "Kansas Place-Names," Rolla was originally named for a pioneer named Reit. The post office, for reasons no one can remember, mistakenly changed the name to Rolla, which is spelled and pronounced the same as Rolla, Mo. According to Rydjord, Rolla "was the phonetic spelling by southerners for Raleigh, North Carolina."

All that aside, you need to stop at the Rolla city park next to U.S. 56 and have your photograph taken next to the Western Kansas Wind Gauge. The gauge is a short length of log chain suspended from a sign with lettering indicating the different western Kansas wind conditions. Dodge City is the windiest city in the United States, with an average wind speed of 14 miles per hour.

The tree-shaded park in Rolla also has picnic tables, a tennis court and a swimming pool if you're looking for a good place to cool your heels. Take a spin through town. I think you'll like the friendly spirit of Rolla.

The next town on U.S. 56 is Wilburton, a vanishing town that has seen better times, and was once home to considerably more residents than today. It was originally named Tice after a Santa Fe railroad official but was later changed to honor its civic-minded postmistress, Mrs. Nellie Wilbur.

At one time Wilburton had two dry-goods stores, two grocery stores, a church, garage, grain elevator, bank, feed yard, florist shop, lumberyard and more than 100 students attending Prairie Flower School about a half-mile north of town.

Despite Wilburton's healthy business district, the population never exceeded more than few hundred sturdy pioneers. Economically it began a downward spiral during the Dust Bowl era.

A colorful pair of outhouses are only part of the structures surrounding Bea's Plantation, a private home north of Wilburton adjacent to the Cimarron National Grasslands.

Signified by a round metal disk is the point where the corners of Kansas, Colorado and Oklahoma intersect. The location, some eight miles west of Elkhart, is also marked with a windmill indicating the juncture of the three states.

A class from Ulysses takes in the view as well as a few pictures from atop Point of Rocks, a historic location on the Santa Fe Trail. Point of Rocks is located on the Cimarron National Grasslands north of Elkhart.

Of the four towns in Morton County, Wilburton is now the smallest, with little more than a railroad sign to mark its existence.

On down the road is Elkhart, the Morton County seat. Named for Elkhart, Ind., it sits just eight miles east of a windmill that marks the spot where Kansas, Oklahoma and Colorado meet.

Elkhart — platted at longitude 101 degrees, 52 feet, 20 inches west, latitude 37 degrees north at an altitude of 3,601.45 feet above sea level — came into being on April 28, 1913.

In 10 days more than 100 business lots were sold. A headline in The Morton County Pioneer, published in Richfield, heralded the town's arrival, saying, "Brand New Town on Santa Fe Road."

Elkhart continues to be a bustling southwestern Kansas community. What was once a treeless, "brand-new town" has grown into a comfortable, tree-lined community with well-kept streets, houses and lawns.

There's a fine motel right on U.S. 56 and several good places to eat, so I recommend that you drive out to Elkhart and plan to stay at either the motel or the campgrounds next to the Cimarron River north of town on K-27. Morton County should be savored, not rushed through.

But enough of this town stuff.

Let's take a drive up K-27 toward the Cimarron River. But before you leave Elkhart you should stop by the U.S. Forest Service office on U.S. 56. They have a handy-dandy auto tour map that takes the worry out of wandering about on open range. There is also a hiking map of the grasslands in case you really want to experience the area.

About two miles north of Elkhart take a left and travel for five miles west. At that point you'll see a guzzler, a device that collects rainfall or heavy dew and stores the water in a tank underneath. There are 84 guzzlers on the grasslands to help provide a continuous water supply for the area's wildlife.

From there the road travels north for 1 1/2 miles to the Cimarron river. On the way you'll pass through the Interstate Oil Field. Although the river may appear to be dry, you don't have to dig deep into the sandy soil to find the river that flows beneath.

Just past the riverbed is a sandy ridge with a small sand dune. Once vegetation grew on the dune, but perpetual exposure to high winds caused what is called a "blowout." The dune areas of the grasslands may vary in size from one to 40 acres.

Along the east-northeast road you'll pass by grazing cattle. More than 10,000 privately owned cattle graze

the grasslands each year under permits from the federal government. At the fork in the road you can travel north to a prairie-dog town and then back south to Point of Rocks, the showcase attraction of the Grasslands.

The formation overlooking the Cimarron River was first noted in the journals of Coronado when he passed through the area in 1541. Three hundred years later it was used as a major landmark on the Santa Fe Trail. It was known as the Cimarron Cut-Off. Looking west from Point of Rocks you can see the Santa Fe Trail markers, limestone posts sticking up at intervals, marking the route of the safer trail to Raton, then Santa Fe.

In 1879 the Beaty brothers — Jap, Jim, Alvin and John — arrived in Morton County from Colorado. Under the leadership of John Beaty, they established the Point of Rocks ranch. During its early years the ranch employed as many as 40 wranglers and four round-up crews.

There are many excellent photographs of the ranch and ranch life at the Morton County museum. In early photographs taken from Point of Rocks the landscape along the river was barren. Now there are thick stands of cottonwoods, willow and salt cedar lining the banks.

During the early morning and late evening hours travelers are likely to see mule deer, elk, antelope, wild turkeys, lesser prairie chickens, pheasant, bobwhite and scaled quail, prairie dogs and coyotes.

In 1914 the Great Flood swept across the valley of the Cimarron and wiped out many ranches, large and small. The Point of Rocks ranch vanished in the swirls of the raging river.

On another sad note in history, the last free-roaming wild bison killed in Kansas was shot by a cowboy as it mingled with a herd of cattle just below the point. It was served for dinner. Middle Springs is 1 1/2 miles east of the cliffs. It provided pioneers a year-round source of water and was another important landmark for travelers.

Continue east to K-27 and cross the highway. About 1 1/2 miles east of K-27 you'll be near the original Santa Fe Trail. Look around. The ruts, etched by wagon wheels in 1834, are still visible.

About seven more miles and you'll be at the Pioneer Memorial Site. The grave site marks the lonely spot where the Brite sisters — Madge, 12, and Merle, 3 — are buried. They were killed during the Great Flood on May 1, 1914. Madge was washed down river from her home, and Merle drowned in her bed.

Follow the road east until it ends at the Wilburton Road where you can turn north for a visit to the once-prosperous town of Richfield, the first Morton County seat. Since you're in no hurry, you really ought to take a spin north and visit Richfield, the town A.T. Spotswood thought would become the main metropolis in Morton County.

It was a busy town at the turn of the century, brimming with businesses, several churches, schools and civic activities. Elkhart, however, had a better location and ended up as the hub of business and county government, something that remains a bone of contention for the remaining Richfield residents.

Back on the Wilburton Road to just past the Cimarron River, take the first right turn (west) and you're on the road back to K-27. If you have a fishing license and your gear you can stop at any of the man-made fishing ponds to the north of the road.

Or, you can head on down to the Cimarron Picnic Ground next to K-27. It has handicapped accessible rest rooms, several fire pits, playground equipment and the most important thing of all — water. It's a wonderful place to pitch a tent and stay the night. A moonless, star-filled Morton County sky is a sight to behold.

Prompted by the yelp of a hen, a 'tom' turkey gobbles for attention while surrounded by a dozen or so other 'toms'. The Kansas wild turkey population exceeds 150,000 birds. The bird was reintroduced into Kansas in the 1960s and 70s.

Did You Know?

Who was Squirrel Tooth Alice?
A Dodge City prostitute

How long did it take the jury to reach a verdict about the Clutter murders written about in "In Cold Blood"?
One hour and 39 minutes

In what Kansas town has the National Junior College Basketball Tournament been played since 1945?
Hutchinson in Reno County

Through what Kansas county does Route 66 pass?
Cherokee County, in the most southeastern corner or Kansas

What Kansas city calls itself the "Little Apple"?
Manhattan in Riley County

Name the only county in Kansas that gave John Kennedy a plurality in the 1960 presidential election.
Ellis

What city in Kansas claims to be the pheasant capital?
Norton in Norton County

When the Kansas Constitution was drawn up, what people were given the right to vote?
White men

What was Concordia native Boston Corbett famous for?
He shot John Wilkes Booth

What native Wichitan played for the Chicago Bears?
Gayle Sayers

Where is the world's largest natural gas field?
Hugoton in Stevens County

Who was the father of college basketball?
Dr. James Naismith of Lawrence

What Rawlins County native drew Smokey the Bear?
Rudolph Wendelin

How many stars are on the state seal?
34

What Kansas town became the first community in the United States to be 100 percent immunized against polio?
Protection in Comanche County in 1957

What was the name given to blacks who migrated to Kansas after the Civil War?
Exodusters

What did the term "jayhawker" originally mean?
Horse thief

What does "ad astra per aspera" mean?
To the stars through difficulties

What were the Astonisher and Paralyzer, Champion Liar and Ginger Snap?
Newspaper names

What Colorado city is named after a Kansas governor?
Denver (Gov. James W. Denver)

When was the cornerstone laid for for the Kansas Capitol?
Oct. 7, 1866

What was the first mineral discovered in Kansas?
Coal

What does the name "Kansas" mean?
"People of the South Wind", "Wind People", "Makes a Breeze Near the Ground"

Victory out of a grand compromise

The merger of five Neosho County towns sparked success for Chanute

Most folks are just waiting for a good excuse to travel somewhere, right? Good, because I have several good excuses for you to visit Neosho County in beautiful southeastern Kansas.

Farmers first settled around Chanute in 1856. They were attracted by the fertile bottomland enriched by the many creeks that feed into the Neosho River.

In the early 1870s, two competing railroad companies were simultaneously laying track that would eventually cross in northern Neosho County. Knowing that a crossing was good for business, a group of promoters conjured up three towns in the hopes that one would emerge as the center of commerce at the crossing. Two years later, after failing to agree on much of anything and weary of fighting, the competing railroads platted a fourth town, and called it Alliance.

It was then that Octavius Chanute, an aeronautical engineer and prominent civic leader, suggested that the five towns combine into one and be assured of winning a railroad line. Everybody must have thought it was a pretty good idea, and to thank Chanute they named the town in his honor.

From 1887 until 1910 the Chanute area enjoyed an oil and gas boom. However, when the boom went bust, the county settled back into agriculture and industry as its primary economic sources.

Since you'll already be in Chanute, you should visit the Martin and Osa Johnson Safari Museum located in the renovated Santa Fe train depot at 111 N. Lincoln Avenue. From 1917-1936 the Johnsons traveled throughout the world, photographing, filming and studying wildlife in East Africa, Borneo and the South Seas. The Johnson's films can be viewed in a 30-seat theater. The museum has one of the finest collections of ceremonial artifacts in the Great Plains. The museum is open from 10 a.m. to 5 p.m. daily and from 1 to 5 p.m. Sunday. For information, call (316) 431-2730.

From Chanute, let's take Santa Fe Street south and visit some small towns in Neosho County. A few miles south of Chanute is the road east to Shaw. As you drive toward Shaw, you'll cross a fine metal-span bridge over the Neosho River.

The county takes its name from this long, undulating body of water. The French referred to it as Le Grand while the Osage Indians called it both Six Bulls and Neosho, which means "water made muddy."

No matter what you call it, this muddy river runs deep and contains flathead catfish of enormous size. If you like to "noodle" (hand-fish illegally for catfish), you would be taking the risk of becoming the "catchee" rather than the "catcher" of the brute-sized catfish found in the Neosho River.

At Shaw was, and I hope still is, the oldest and most unusual Kansas state historical marker I've found during my travels in Kansas. This aging sign is unlike other state markers because it is supported by cedar tree trunks rather than the more traditional metal posts. This marker needs to be restored, not replaced.

It tells the story of Mission Neosho, the first Indian mission and school in Kansas. Established by missionary Benton Pixley in 1824, the school was located about 1/3 mile west of Shaw. It seems that some of the Osage Indians and the Indian agent didn't much care for Pixley and his school, so they took to disrupting church meetings and discouraged Indian children from attending the school. In 1829 the school was abandoned.

In 1884, A.B. Canville opened a trading post a short distance from the historical marker. And nearby, on Sept. 29, 1865, the Osage signed a treaty with the U.S. government, giving up much of their reserve in Kansas. A lot of interesting things happened around the marker, and the local folks would be happy to fill you in on the details.

Behind the marker is the oak tree shaded home of the pastor of the small but homey Shaw Christian Church. If you're interested in an old-fashioned church service, you can attend Sunday services at 10:45 a.m.

After Shaw, travel to Stark in the northeast corner of the county. Originally it was called Grant Center, but the name was changed to Stark to avoid any possible confusion with Grand Center. Frank Leighton, postmaster at Grant Center, suggested the town be named after his birthplace in Stark County, Ill.

It's not a big town by any means, but it's doing well enough for the Stark State Bank to have a revolving time and temperature sign. The Town and Country Cafe across the street is a good place to stop for lunch, and rumor has it that it's a Mecca of sorts for bluegrass musicians. Stark, unlike most Kansas towns, still allows you to park in the middle of the street.

Two miles south is the town of Kimball, named for C.H. Kimball, a Parsons politician and military man. The town is almost gone save for a few families and a church. Along the main street are the remnants of a general store, now overgrown by trees and bushes. It is the only sign of Kimball's economic past.

From Kimball, you can take back roads to Erie, the Neosho County seat with an Iroquois name. The attractive, original county courthouse is gone, the only remnant of the old structure being the red brick county jail behind the new county building.

The '60s were an unfortunate time for Kansas county courthouses.

Restoration wasn't a common thing then, and many were razed. The Neosho County Courthouse was a victim of that time. A painting of the stately old courthouse hangs in the lobby of the new building.

Erie is an interesting town to drive around in because of the unusual mixture of house styles. The city park and swimming pool offer cool, shaded respite from the summer heat.

St. Paul is our next stop. If you like magnificent structures, the St. Francis de Hieronymo Church will fit the bill quite nicely. Dedicated May 11, 1884, the church is impressive in size and elegance. The interior is breathtaking, and the garden to the east has a nice series of walkways that take you through the 14 Stations of the Cross.

St. Paul was originally named Osage Mission, then called Catholic Mission, but the name was later changed to St. Paul in honor of St. Paul of the Cross, founder of the Passionist Order.

East and south of St. Paul is the Neosho State Wildlife Area. Critters looking for a good place to hide will find ample refuge in the 2,976 acres provided for them in the wildlife area. October through March is the best time to see large populations of migrating ducks and snow geese.

About seven miles south and east of the wildlife area is a little gem of a lake called Neosho State Fishing Lake.

I never stopped to ask if the sign was true, but it's obvious that the folks in South Mound have a wonderful sense of humor and are willing to share it with anyone who takes the time to visit this small town in Neosho County.

Locally known as McKinley Lake, the lily pad-ringed body of water is a fine place to fish, camp, picnic or take pictures.

Two miles north and west of the lake is a very small town with a big sense of humor. As you enter South Mound from the south, a spiffy metal sign greets visitors:

"South Mound America, Home of 35 people, one dope-headed welfare case and one old grouch."

From South Mound travel south about three miles then west seven miles to Parsons City Lake, a fine 980-acre fishing hole. Many of the lakes in southeast Kansas are excellent panfish fisheries featuring bluegill, red-eared sunfish and warmouth. On the southwest edge of the lake is the Sportsman Shelter Camping Area. The area has camper hookups, a large shelter for gatherings, and an excellent playground and softball diamond.

By this time, your daylight hours will be pretty well shot. But if you have the time, stop at Galesburg, said to be named after Galesburg, Ill., or Thayer, a town that takes its name from railroad financier Nathaniel Thayer. And lastly there is Earlton, established in 1884 and named for a settler known only as Mr. Earle.

A great blue heron stands silently in the shallow waters of Neosho Wildlife Area near St. Paul.

Following the journey of a meandering prairie stream

Surprises await those who follow the many twists and turns of the South Fork of the Ninnescah

Ever wonder where a river begins?

On a Kansas state transportation map the South Fork of the Ninnescah River is a thin blue line beginning southwest of Cullison in Pratt County. It ends where the blue line merges with the North Fork of the Ninnescah, south and west of Garden Plain in Sedgwick County, a little more than 60 miles from where it first bubbles out of the sandy soil of Pratt County.

But in that relatively short distance, the South Fork grows from a dry gulch that flows under the sandy prairie to a river several hundred feet wide — a clear waterway teeming with life, lined with cottonwoods, willow, and ash.

This day trip is a journal of observations and images made while chronicling a rivulet as it grows into a river. The solution to following any body of water is to figure where it's heading, then crisscross the countryside on county roads until you find the next bridge. In the process of following the river, feel free to wander the back roads and explore the small towns along or near the river's edge.

Bridge No. 1: Visually, the South Fork begins in open prairie, a sandy-colored swath winding east and passing under the road to Coats, south of U.S. 54. Sand plum thickets line its banks here. Berries, red and full as a setting sun, hang in profusion. Somewhere, several miles to the west in a rancher's field, is

the real point of origin. Leaving it a mystery seems appropriate.

Bridge No. 2: Three miles east of the dry gulch, the open prairie gives way to cathedral-like cottonwoods lining a still-dry riverbed. Evidence of recent rains can be seen in lines of surge-formed sand waves; dried leaves adorn the top of each wave, slightly darkened from residual moisture.

Bridge No. 3: Clear water is flowing now. A mile or so west of Pratt, somewhere on private land, the river has surfaced to begin its long and rambling trek to the Mississippi River delta and the Gulf of Mexico. At this point it's only 5 feet wide and 5 inches deep, a clear, quiet beginning to a powerful and important finish.

Bridge No. 4: South Main Street in Pratt. In the mile from the last bridge, the river has become deeper and wider. Under a fallen willow, five large carp angle themselves into the current, moving slowly as they forage in the aquatic vegetation. Bright yellow flowers dotted against rich green leaves cover the water in an eddy pool south of the bridge.

Bridge No. 5: Let's stop for a short visit to the Kansas Department of Wildlife and Parks headquarters, which parallels the river. Wildlife and Parks fishery biologists think a lot of the South Fork. According to their surveys the river has good populations of black bass, green sunfish, crappie, channel catfish and flathead catfish.

The river's banks are now thick with cottonwood, willow and ash trees, home and habitat for wild turkeys, raccoons, beavers, muskrats, mink, white-tailed deer and the occasional mule deer.

In the course of only a few miles, the South Fork has begun to take on its own character and diversity of wildlife. A stop at the Wildlife and Parks Exhibit Hall across from the headquarters is well worth the visit. Take your time with the exhibits; an hour is enough time to go through the building and learn about Kansas fisheries and wildlife, and their varied habitats. South of the exhibit hall, next to the river, is a park with picnic tables, rest rooms, and plenty of riverbank.

Bridge No. 6: The river heads north now, passing under U.S. 54 for the first time. Its water, clear and fast, makes the going hard for a snapping turtle moving against the current. Occasionally, the turtle takes refuge behind a rock, a brief respite from the current. A bobwhite quail calls out from its hiding place in a nearby sand plum thicket.

Bridge No. 7: Under a bridge, just south of the Waldeck elevator, a small brown water snake glides alongside the bank. Moving with the current, its slender body reflects the water's rhythm as it moves onto the cattail-lined bank.

Bridge No. 8: Cairo, a nice town. On our way to the river, a half-mile north of town, two horses eat their way through a rain-damaged milo field. Bright red cannas line a garden in front of two white frame houses.

From Pratt to Cairo the river has widened from 5 to 50 feet. It has also become shallower and faster as it ripples over the sand, twisting and turning through the sandy prairie. A pile of charred wood adorns the north bank, evidence perhaps of a night fishing trip or a lovers' interlude. Cottonwood leaves dance to the tune of the south wind, their broad, shiny leaves shimmering in the sunlight.

It's mighty nice out here, but it's time to leave the river for a short while. East on U.S. 54, I glance north to the river at each mile. My philosophy is to always leave something unknown for another time.

Bridge No. 9: The sign says "Welcome to Cunningham, founded in 1885." I watch as two old men help each other walk the sidewalk toward Harold's Place. "Hot Beer and Poor Service," Harold's sign proudly boasts. Looks like a good place to stop for lunch.

It's cool and dark in Harold's, and the people are friendly to a stranger. While he eats a spiced sausage, a young man at the bar talks about three local boys who will soon go into the Air Force. Another man mentions an

11-pound flathead recently caught in a good "little hole" under a fallen cottonwood on the South Fork. Best fishin' is near the Turon Road, but it, like all of the land surrounding the river, is private; access is by permission only.

North of town, beneath the Turon Road bridge, the South Fork has evolved into a river of some width and presence; it's 100 feet wide now. Its sandbars take on interesting shapes and textures, mirroring the action of the water above them. Sand plum thickets, Russian olive trees and prickly pear cacti sprinkled along the banks round out the scene against a light blue sky. Mourning doves are thick along the banks.

An important part of field observation is to look for what is different from the last mile. If you look for the same things, that's all you'll see and you'll miss the rest.

Bridge No. 10: South now, under U.S. 54, the river spills from its banks, creating marshes that support waterfowl. Two great blue heron stand stark-still, waiting for the precise moment to spear the small fish swimming at their feet. We have entered the Byron Walker Wildlife Area on the northern edge of the Gypsum Hills.

Within the 4,000-acre Byron Walker Wildlife Area are multiple points of public access to the South Fork. This will be the only opportunity you have

to walk or float the river for up to
seven miles. Use this area to its fullest
advantage for exploring the river. Maps
are available at the wildlife area headquarters on the south side of the road,
directly across from Kingman State
Fishing Lake.

Bridge No. 11: The river crosses
north here and parallels the state fishing lake, the only body of water of any
size on its 60-mile journey. This sweet,
shallow water fishing lake is nestled
into a peaceful wooded area dotted
with picnic tables. Its west and north
banks are lined with lilies in full
bloom. Nice habitat for largemouth
bass and panfish and not a bad spot for
an easy chair and a good book.
Kingman is also one of the few Kansas
lakes with northern pike.

*Characterized by its
clear water and sand-
bars, the South Fork of
the Ninnescah flows
southeast near Cairo.
The Ninnescah means
"clear water."*

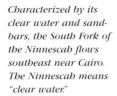

*Petite wildflowers
dance along the edge
of the South Fork of
the Ninnescah as it
courses through Pratt
County.*

Bridge No. 12: Leaving the lake area, the river crosses under U.S. 54 for the last time as it begins its journey southward.

Bridge No. 13: Kingman, second and last town on the river. The South Fork must have caused some trouble here at one time, because its width is controlled by levees. From a meandering river, it has become straight and narrow, conforming to a channel and needing to rise at least 12 feet to leave its banks. There's plenty of people activity along the river's edge. The Kingman County Fair is in full swing, but the river pays it no mind as it quietly slips by the packed activity center.

Bridge No. 14: After leaving Kingman, the river becomes less convenient, returning to its twisting, turning pattern. Accessibility is reduced because there are fewer bridges. I am now traveling on land where roads aren't built on a square-mile grid, but rather according to the river's whim.

Bridge No. 15: Murdock, named for the founder of The Wichita Eagle. It's a small town, remarkably well kept and flourishing for its size. From the bridge, south of town, two young women can be seen downstream sunbathing on lawn chairs in the middle of the shallow river. It's private land, but they have permission to enjoy the cooling river on a hot summer day. To the west of the bridge is Camp Mennoscah, a popular church camp.

Bridge No. 16: It's the last bridge before the South and North Forks of the Ninnescah converge on private land. It's time to find the landowner who can take me to where the rivers meet. I stop a farmer who is plowing near the road. Turns out that he owns the land where the two rivers meet and doesn't mind taking me there. He asks only that I not mention his name or the location.

After a rough ride across a pasture we stop near the North Fork, take off our boots, roll up our pant legs and wade into the river. The North Fork doesn't run as hard as the South Fork, primarily because its flow is controlled by the dam at Cheney Reservoir.

Many Kansas rivers and streams have fallen victim to reservoirs, lakes and watershed dams which help reduce downstream flooding but eventually kill living waterways because their flows are reduced to a slow, turbid crawl.

The North Fork is still and dark as we walk the quarter mile to the confluence. Carp, lovers of slow moving water, swirl at our feet, disturbed from their feeding by human intrusion. The river becomes deeper as we approach the confluence. Our rolled-up pants are to no avail in the now waist-deep water. Silty sand squishes up between our toes as we approach the clear, fast water of the South Fork.

Finally, we step into the cool, swift current of the South Fork as it is joined by its smaller, more turbid, northern counterpart. There, the rivers blend then flow south to eventually merge with the Arkansas River near Whitman in Sumner County.

A large sandbar has formed where the two rivers meet. Footprints of a person wearing sandals and evidence of a camp fire wait for the next high water to erase their brief presence on this clear prairie river.

Was it worth the trip? You bet.

Did You Know?

The first forward pass in football history was thrown in December 1905. What two schools were playing at the time?
Washburn University and Fairmount College

Who as a child was burned so badly he wasn't expected to walk, but set a world record in 1938 for the mile?
Glenn Cunningham of Elkhart in Morton County

What Kansas woman became the first female mayor in the world?
Susanna Salter of Argonia (Sumner County) in 1887

Who is credited with creating our state motto?
Kansas Sen. John James Ingalls

What was the name of the historic statehouse cottonwood tree that was removed in October 1984?
"Old General"

What church established the first mission in Kansas?
The Methodist Church established the Shawnee Mission

What is the highest point in Kansas?
Mount Sunflower — 4,039 feet in Wallace County

Who was the first Kansas state governor?
Charles Robinson

Where was the original "Little House on the Prairie"?
12 miles southeast of Independence in Montgomery County

Which one of Kansas' 105 counties is named for a woman?
Barton County, named for Clara Barton, Civil War nurse and founder of the American Red Cross

Who was the first governor impeached in Kansas?
Charles Robinson, Kansas' first governor

Name the autobiographical novel about a boy growing up in Fort Scott.
"The Learning Tree" by Gordon Parks, photographer/writer and Fort Scott native

Name the Kansas native who wrote "Picnic," "Dark at the Top of the Stairs" and "Come Back Little Sheba".
Willian Inge of Independence in Montgomery County

What Kansas author first gained national notice with an anti-Populist piece titled "What's the Matter With Kansas?"
William Allen White of Emporia in Lyons County

What is the origin of the name, Beecher Bible and Rifle Church?
In the years just before the Civil War, Henry Ward Beecher shipped rifles labeled as Bibles to a church in the town of Wabaunsee in northern Wabaunsee County. The church continues to hold services each Sunday.

What are the dimensions of the state?
411 miles long, 208 miles wide

What promise (later violated) did the Missouri Compromise make to Kansans in 1820?
To forever prohibit slavery in Kansas

What does Topeka mean?
"A good place to dig potatoes"

Name at least two movies filmed in Kansas.
"Picnic," "Paper Moon," "Gypsy Moth," "The Day After" and "Kansas"

Who played in the first nighttime football game in Kansas?
Fairmount College (now Wichita State University) and Cooper College (now Sterling College)

Top of the morning in north central Kansas

Sunrise at Coronado Heights is the springboard for this journey

OK, folks, let's roll for a day.

You know — get your map, pack a picnic, load up the car and head down the road.

Timing is an important part of any day trip. You need to allow yourself enough time to get from Wichita or wherever you live to our first stop, Coronado Heights. And it's best if you're there before sunrise.

From Wichita take I-135 north to just past Lindsborg. There's a sign indicating where to leave the highway, so pay attention. The exit will take you to old U.S. 81, then back south for a mile or so. Watch for the Coronado Heights sign on your right and head west at the turn.

Coronado Heights, also known as Spanish Buttes, is a mighty fine place to start your day about a half-hour before sunrise. The cool morning air, heavy with the moisture and the fragrance of prairie grasses, moves up the slopes to greet you. The view isn't bad either.

It's a unique experience to climb the irregular stairway to the roof of the shelter house, the Dakota limestone structure that marks this Smoky Hill prominence, also known as Spanish Buttes.

The distinctive shelter sits on 16 1/2 acres of land. It was built in 1936 by the Works Progress Administration. Arrayed like gun turrets on a ship, there are 15 picnic tables and fireplaces facing out from the edge of the cliffs surrounding the shelter. Inside the shelter is a large room with stone tables and an oversized fireplace. If you don't do anything but enjoy the sunrise, it will have been worth the stop.

After enjoying the sunrise, you can always swing two miles south into Lindsborg for a fine breakfast, or you can head on up I-135, past Salina, to the Minneapolis exit. (Minneapolis, by the way, is where George Washington Carver attended high school. He later invented more than 300 uses for the peanut). At that point you'll be very close to a geology oddity that begs the question: How the heck did these funny-looking rocks get here?

"ROCK CITY... A Natural Wonder," the brochure reads. And a natural wonder it is. What you will see is not a common sight. These odd formations of

Rock City, located south of Minneapolis, is home to dozens of "concretions", rare and unusual formations of rocks unearthed by the erosion caused by thousands of years of wind and rain.

rock are located 2 1/2 miles southwest of Minneapolis. They're in a strip about 125 feet wide by 1,700 feet long.

Funny-looking things, these 200 or so Dakota sandstone concretions. At first, one might assume that receding glaciers deposited the large orbs while melting their way north, but naaaaah, that's too simple an answer. According to popular geological belief, these concretions are the result of millenniums of rock growth, much like a pearl grows around a small piece of sand.

This natural growth process is thought to have started with a large fossil or extra-large piece of sand that served as a nucleus. Slow flowing underground water containing calcium carbonate was deposited on the nucleus, causing a slow but steady cementation of materials that eventually grew into these large formations.

Although examples of this phenomenon are found throughout the world, these concretions are the largest. This geological freak show must be seen to be believed. Postcards and memorabilia are available at a small gift shop owned by a private, non-profit corporation. There's a per car admission, but what the heck. Where else can you see something like this? Tanzania, maybe?

From Rock City I'd recommend that you take the county blacktop straight north from Minneapolis to K-41, then left to Delphos. This Ottawa County town was named by its first postmaster for his hometown in Ohio. Its small business district is built on a square surrounding a city park.

History, according to The Wichita Eagle archives, has it that on Nov. 2, 1971, a spaceship landed on a farm near Delphos. A somewhat stunned 16-year-old boy walked into his house and told his parents that a flying saucer had landed near him while he was tending the sheep. The family then ran out into the backyard and saw a bright light climbing into the sky. The boy's dog was blinded for five days.

Supposedly no vegetation — save for strange, hardened mushrooms that grew to about an inch high then disappeared — has grown on the spot where the UFO landed. Newspaper reports say that the ring on the ground formed by the spaceship was so radioactive that it ran the needle clear off the scale on a Geiger counter.

Ask around — maybe the story is true. Heck, it was in the newspaper.

From Delphos take another county blacktop straight north to U.S. 24. Turn left toward Beloit, the Mitchell County seat originally known as Willow Springs.

Be sure to tour the streets of Beloit. Visit the interior of the massive St. John's Catholic Church, the Al Street Home and the magnificent Mitchell County Courthouse. All are on the National Register of Historic Places.

And don't forget the Little Red Schoolhouse; it's a National Monument and is affiliated with the National Library of Congress.

The Beloit City Park on the south end of town is a fine place to relax during the heat of the day or have a picnic lunch next to the Solomon River as it runs down a gently sloping spillway then meanders out of town toward the dam at Minneapolis. It's worth the visit.

On to Glen Elder, a fine small town by a dam site, and then to Cawker City, the home of a silly but challenging hobby. Glen Elder is the "Gateway to Waconda Reservoir," one of the finest white bass, channel catfish and walleye fishing holes in Kansas. The long dam that runs south from Glen Elder is an easy place to fish from during the April walleye spawn. And if you keep heading south you'll pass through Tipton and Hunter. But that's another day trip.

The state park is slowly being refurbished after the catastrophic floods of 1993, a 500-year flood event that destroyed virtually all of the park facilities, and much of the vegetation and trees in the popular 13,000-acre wildlife area.

The area has rebounded nicely and the wildlife area continues to provide upland game hunters with some of the best pheasant hunting in Kansas. Stop

at the state park office, located just west of Glen Elder, to pick up a map of the park and wildlife area.

Cawker City, just down the road from Glen Elder, seems like a quiet little town. You would never guess that this small hamlet on the edge of Waconda Lake became balled up in a twine controversy in the late 1980s. It's strange, but true.

For years, Cawker Citians proudly laid claim to having the world's largest ball of twine, at least until that ill-fated day when a stranger from Minnesota stepped out of the shadows, measured the Cawker Citians' revered ball of twine, and turned into the grinch that stole their fame.

Francis Johnson, the Minnesotan, is not a name to bring up in Cawker City. For it was he who, for a time, took the title away from local hero and ultimate twine gatherer Frank Stoeber. Both men started their twineballing for similar reasons in 1953, but it was Johnson who briefly prevailed, causing Cawker City to change its sign, "World's Largest Ball of Twine" to "One of the World's Largest Balls of Twine."

The Cawker Citians, not to be bested by some "you betcha" hooligan, gathered as much twine as they could and reclaimed the title of "World's Largest Ball of Twine." They're so sure that they'll maintain the record that they've built a brand-new shelter for

the ball, and put up two new signs proclaiming their proper place in twine gathering history. Stoeber would be proud.

For those of you who love statistics, the ball of twine weighs 14,687 pounds, is 40 feet, 3 inches in circumference and contains 5,874,000 feet of twine, which is equal to 1,113 miles in length.

On to Downs, home of the Dragons, then north on K-181 to Lebanon and the center of it all. Don't just pass through Downs. Be sure to stop in at the bait shop/indoor archery range on the highway or the downtown cafe to get an up-to-date fishing report on Waconda ("great spirit") Lake. The lake is better known to anglers as Glen Elder.

North of Lebanon, in Smith County, is the geographic center of the 48 contiguous states. Big deal, you say? Well, it is a big deal. After all, Kansas is the

Glen Elder Reservoir, State Park and Wildlife Area located in Mitchell County between the towns of Glen Elder, Cawker City and Downs, are hot spots for anglers, campers and hunters. Night fishing for white bass is a popular summertime activity.

If you are a channel cat angler then Glen Elder Reservoir is the place to be, especially in mid-October.

Heart of America, the Hub of the Nation and the Crossroads of North America.

You can prove it to yourself and all your disbelieving friends by driving two miles north and a little west of Lebanon. There you'll find a monument and plaque on a skinny pyramid. Don't forget to take a picture or two while you're there, and to visit the small chapel adjacent to the pyramid.

In Osborne County, about 40 miles straight south of the geographic center of the 48 states, is the geodetic center of North America, or the point on which the surface of North America would balance if it were of uniform thickness.

The center is on Meade's Ranch and is nothing more than a simple bronze marker with cross hairs. The marker identifies it as the primary station from which all surveys are calculated for a sixth of the world's surface.

None of these places we've visited is going to raise your adrenaline level, or shout in your face, or, most importantly, charge you a big admission. But if you haven't been there or seen this part of north central Kansas, then I'm certain that you're in for a treat.

Did You Know?

What is the state tree?
Cottonwood

What is the state flower?
Sunflower

What is the name of the school that was established in 1884 to educate Indians and where is it?
Haskell Institute, Lawrence

What president signed a bill that made Kansas a state on Jan. 29, 1861?
James Buchanan

How was the meadowlark selected as the Kansas state bird?
Schoolchildren chose it in an election sponsored by the Audubon Society

Who was the first black woman to win an Academy Award?
Hattie McDaniel, a Kansan, for "Gone With the Wind"

What are some other nicknames for Kansas besides Sunflower State?
Cyclone State, Garden of the West, Jayhawker State, Grasshopper State

What Chapman native piloted the Columbia space shuttle?
Gen. Joe Engle

How many years did it take to build our state Capitol?
37

Kansas was the first state to ratify what amendment?
The 15th, which gives blacks the right to vote

Who was the sage of Emporia?
William Allen White

Who was the world-renowned Wichita Indian artist?
Blackbear Bosin, creator of the Keeper of the Plains statue

What stagecoach enterprise advertised in 1865 "trips leaving daily from Atchison to Denver" with a scheduled travel time of eight days?
Butterfield Overland Dispatch

Where is the geographical center of the continental United States?
Near Lebanon in Smith County

What Kansas town was the bison hide center of the United States?
Dodge City in Ford County

Where is the official state fair held?
Hutchinson in Reno County

Rena Milner was the first female city manager in the country. Where did she serve in 1928?
Kinsley in Edwards County

When was the first official Thanksgiving in Kansas?
Nov. 20, 1856

Name the four species of poisonous snakes in Kansas.
Prairie rattlesnake, timber rattlesnake, Massasagua rattlesnake and copperhead

Where was Carry Nation from?
Medicine Lodge in Barber County

What was Gov. Alf Landon's most noteworthy accomplishment besides running for president against Roosevelt in '36?
He balanced the state budget

When did the Kansas Turnpike open?
1956

What kind of winter wheat did the Mennonites bring to Kansas from Russia that helped make Kansas the "breadbasket of America"?
Turkey Red

Northwest Kansas: The Land of Many Surprises

Let's spend a day or two on U.S. 36

Far northwestern Kansas: What a mighty fine place it is, full of friendly folks, beautiful terrain and lots of history. Heck, let's go there for the weekend.

From Wichita take I-135 north to I-70, then west to Goodland — a good place to start. Most of you probably have driven right past Goodland on the way to or from Colorado. Big mistake.

Goodland, the Sherman County seat, was founded in the late 1880s and named for Goodland, Ind. — the city where one of the major stockholders in the town company came from. According to "Kansas Place-Names," by John Rydjord, the name Goodland was used to promote the place as a "good land" to settle.

To this day most everyone will agree that the land is good but sometimes high and dry. According to Rydjord's book, a rainmaker was once hired to make sure the town lived up to its name. The rains came in torrents, so heavy that parts of Nebraska were flooded. The damage to the north was so great that Nebraska is reported to have sued the rainmaker for an excess of success.

Today Goodland is a prosperous town and home to a fine historical repository called the High Plains Museum. The museum, at 1717 Cherry Street in downtown Goodland has, in addition to other neat stuff, a replica of the first patented helicopter built in the United States. It was put together by two Sherman County machinists in 1909-1910.

The museum also has an exhibit featuring prehistoric Indians as well as information on pioneer sod homes, where they were located and a replica of a sod house.

Admission is free, and it's open 9 a.m. to 5 p.m. Monday through Saturday, Sunday 1 p.m. to 5 p.m. For more information, call (785) 899-4595 or (785) 899-3351.

From Goodland we're going to venture south to visit Mount Sunflower in Wallace County. Take K-27 south for about 15 miles. A small brown sign on the right (west) side of the road directs you to drive an additional nine miles west and six miles south from K-27. It's a good all-weather road and there's a reasonable chance that you might see an antelope, so take it and go.

As you approach the highest point in Kansas you won't find a remarkable geological feature to climb, just an ever-so-slight incline from the county

Visitors to the Arikaree Breaks, located north of St. Francis, pick wildflowers and a species of sage unique to the extreme northwest corner of Kansas.

road to the crest, some 4,039 feet above the plains. Mount Sunflower is a marvelous place to visit, something every Kansan should do. The site is on private land but the owners have been generous enough to allow the public unlimited access to the summit.

A brightly colored sign stands guard next to the entrance gate. When you reach the summit there is a registration book in a mailbox. Be sure everyone in your group signs in, and take a minute or two to read the comments of other visitors. Throughout the book are dozens of signatures from members of the High-Pointers Club, an active bunch of folks who endeavor to summit every state's highest point.

Here are a few of the comments from folks who visited the summit.

Clarence Anderson, July 11, 1990, New Strawn, Kan. — "Because it is here and I'm 85 years old and I could drive to the Summit."

Rudy Vadowell, July 11, 1990, Holland, Mich. — "Trying to reach the highest point in 30 states, this is number 22. Another beautiful day."

Patty and Dick Jones, July 13, 1990, Wichita, Kan. — "Potential ski trip— wish there had been snow here."

Be sure to take a lot of photographs and roll some videotape while you're there — it's something to share with your friends. Who knows, maybe it will encourage them to stop by for a visit.

There is also a covered picnic shelter next to Kansas' highest point. Another fine gesture from the folks who own the land.

When your visit is complete drive east one mile, and instead of going north five miles and then east to K-27, take the road north all the way to Kanorado. You'll drive straight north except for one dog-leg left, then right, as you cross the Wallace/Sherman County line.

It's a nice drive that will take you on a backroad journey paralleling the Kansas-Colorado border until you eventually cross the South Fork of the Republican River. From there the same road angles northeast along the river to St. Francis, the Cheyenne County seat. You'll cross the river twice before the road drops you onto U.S. 36, just west of St. Francis. It's a fine drive that should give you an opportunity to see wild turkeys and deer if you're there early or late in the day.

For the less adventuresome, take the road from Mount Sunflower back to K-27, then head north to where it intersects with U.S.36 at Wheeler. Turn left and make the short drive to St. Francis.

Cheyenne County is the first and the smallest, population-wise, of 13 counties that U.S. 36 passes through before it leaves Kansas at Elwood. The clear, tree-lined Republican River runs over sand as it meanders northeast from Colorado, through St. Francis, exiting Kansas near Benkelman, Neb.

St. Francis was not named for a Catholic saint but for Frances Emerson, the wife of one of the town's founders (the masculine form of the name was chosen). A civic-minded, religious woman, "Fanny," as she was called, was revered by local folks for her saintly behavior. The town was named in her honor.

St. Francis also has the honor of registering the coldest temperature ever recorded in Kansas in August, a chilly 33 degrees in 1910. On average, Cheyenne County is the coolest county in Kansas. The average July temperature hovers right at 77 degrees and a January average is 28 degrees.

If you visit Cheyenne County in August you might be lucky enough to be there on the weekend of the county fair. Years ago Cheyenne County fair officials decided that it was too expensive to bring in a carnival so they began to shop around and buy rides such as a ferris wheel, tilt-a-whirl, merry-go-round, etc., from carnivals that were either going out of business or updating their equipment.

The result is a wholesome, community-run carnival where no one shouts at passers-by and everybody knows you by your name. As one fairgoer put it, "You can let your kids run loose and not worry. It's a nice feeling." St. Francis would have been a perfect setting for a Norman Rockwell painting.

NORTHWEST KANSAS | 105

In downtown St. Francis are the county courthouse and one of the most attractive and acoustically effective band shells I've seen or heard. What makes it different from most band shells is the circular concrete seating arrangement that surrounds the front of the shell. The unique shape helps to reverberate sounds from the stage. It also serves to collect sounds from great distances. I could hear the normal conversation of two tennis players from a half-block away.

And while you're in St. Francis don't forget to visit the Cheyenne County Museum on U.S. 36. The museum is open Monday through Friday from 1 p.m. to 4 p.m. or by calling (785) 332-2809 or (785) 332-3119. There are several brochures, featuring local points of interest, at the museum or downtown at the Chamber of Commerce.

For a nice side trip take K-27 north from town for about a mile to the Cherry Creek Encampment. My good friend Tobe Zweygardt, the definitive Cheyenne County historian, has created and assembled an interesting set of icons depicting several historic events.

A 1/4-inch thick piece of steel cut into the shape of a bison represents the last wild bull bison killed in Cheyenne County. One of Zweygardt's hefty signs explains that the bison was shot by Sam Ferguson and other homesteaders on April 25, 1887.

Hanging next to that sign is another explaining a massacre. It reads: "In memory of the Cheyenne and Arapaho Indians, survivors of the 29 Nov. 1864 massacre at Sand Creek, Colorado, who fled to this Cherry Creek Valley, remaining until joined by forces of other plains tribes for an attack at Julesburg, Colo., 7 Jan. 1865."

On a ridge to the west is a large metal cutout of an Indian on horseback. Other items include a metal teepee, several metal cutouts of prairie dogs behind the bison and a mailbox with a visitor registration book. Don't forget to sign in before you leave. Tobe would sure appreciate it if you did.

If you're really into backroad adventure, get out your DeLorme Kansas Atlas and Gazetteer and find the Arikaree River in the far northwest corner of page 15. Use the book or the "Self-Guided Driving Tour" pamphlet from the museum to guide you toward Devil's Gap and Devil's Canyon, and the Arikaree River. You'll still be in Kansas, but you'll be within shouting distance of Colorado. Just across the state line, into Colorado about 25 miles, is the site of the Battle of Beecher's Island.

It was a six-day battle that took place in September 1868 between the 50 civilian scouts under the command of Maj. George Forsyth and Lt. Fred Beecher and several hundred renegade Indians led by Chief Roman Nose, a

Northern Cheyenne. The Indians had Forsyth and his men pinned down on an island in the Arikaree River.

Roman Nose was killed on the second day of the battle. When the Indians finally withdrew, six of Forsyth's men were dead, including Beecher. More than half the defenders were wounded in the battle, including Forsyth who sustained four wounds. A memorial marks the battleground.

If you're really looking for a road with a view then take the paved road straight north out of St. Francis. The pavement ends shortly after you cross the Republican River. Keep heading north-northeast, but don't take the turn to the east. It's a fine roller coaster drive, with historic highlights indicated on the "Self-Guided Driving Tour." The drive will eventually drop you into Nebraska, but not before dazzling your senses with a magnificent view of the Arikaree Breaks.

You won't see the Breaks coming, but you'll know it when you're there as you crest a hill and they unfold before you from east to west. Stop and soak up the landscape. It's the only one of its kind in Kansas and you've got the cat bird seat.

When you've used up all your film, take the road back south to St. Francis, then head east to Bird City, a small town with two signs to greet you. Get used to being welcomed as you travel

Part of the rich tableau that is Kansas is the cabin where Dr. Brewster Higley wrote "My Western Home," a song that would later become "Home on the Range," the Kansas state song. The cabin, which is open to the public, is located nine miles north of U.S. 36 at Athol.

U.S. 36. There's a lot of community pride in Kansas and good reason for it.

The first sign, "Bird City—641 Friendly People Live Here" is immediately followed by another sign that reads "Lindbergh's Playground, Bird City, Kansas." The second sign also has a nice drawing of Lucky Lindy just to make sure you remember who he was.

As a young aeronaut, Charles Lindbergh used to barnstorm out of Bird City. And it was one of the places he chose to visit after completing his historic transatlantic flight in 1927.

Irish Catholics founded Bird City in 1885 and originally named it Bird Town, to honor Benjamin Bird, a local newspaper editor. Take Bird Avenue south into town and look around some. Downtown on Fourth Street is an attractive stone building labeled City Hall. It's now the home of the Mary L. Gritten Library. On the west side of town is a very nice city park

Tobe Zweygardt is a talented folk artist, historian, storyteller, and a lifelong resident of Cheyenne County in the northwest corner of Kansas. Zweygardt's metal sculptures of a bison, prairie dog, a teepee and an Indian on horseback are part of the historical display he created north of St. Francis on K-27. The display depicts the last wild bison killed in Cheyenne County and the massacre of Arapahoe and Cheyenne Indians at Sand Creek in nearby Colorado.

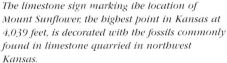

The limestone sign marking the location of Mount Sunflower, the highest point in Kansas at 4,039 feet, is decorated with the fossils commonly found in limestone quarried in northwest Kansas.

with sheltered picnic tables and a good playground.

After your Bird City visit return to U.S. 36, a once famous highway that was one of the main routes from the upper midwest to the Rockies, or as one sign says, "U.S. 36, the Fastest Route from Denver to Indianapolis."

The next town east is McDonald, in Rawlins County. If you've not had the opportunity to visit an old-time grocery store then you should stop at McDonald Grocery. While you're in the small downtown area there are several other old buildings that deserve a once-over.

Time for a little backroad trek.

About eight miles east of McDonald, at the Beardsley turnoff, take the all-weather road south into the valley of the North Fork of Beaver Creek. Take that road south for four miles, east for 1/2 mile, north for one mile, east for one mile, north for 1 1/2 miles, east for 1/2 mile, then north for 1 1/2 miles to U.S. 36. Now, wasn't that fun?

It's a beautiful valley filled with wildlife, and it's worth the side trip. If you take your time, and you really should, you're likely to scare up the herd of mule deer that make a living along the creek bottom. Trust me. If you don't take these side trips you'll never see what the countryside has to offer.

Our next stop is Atwood, named for the son of town founder J.M. Matheny,

and the Rawlins County seat. During the Hayden administration a large sign welcomed visitors to: "Atwood, Home of Kansas Governor Mike Hayden and His Family."

Atwood, much like St. Francis, is an attractive, tree-shaded town nestled into the valley of Beaver Creek. Unlike most of the county courthouses found in towns along U.S. 36, the Rawlins County building, completed in 1907, is a red brick affair with a spire to top it off.

In front of the courthouse, on one of the business district's grass medians, is a bison sculpture created by Pete Felten, a well-known sculptor from Hays. Four of Felten's sculptures, depicting Amelia Earhart, President Dwight Eisenhower, Arthur Capper and William Allen White, are permanently housed in the rotunda of the state Capitol.

Atwood High School, Home of the Buffaloes, sits atop the hill a block or so from the courthouse. Both St. Francis and Atwood chose to build their high schools on a hill on the east side of town, at the end of their business districts.

Tucked into the north side of town is Atwood Lake, a man-made lake formed by a dam on Beaver Creek. The tree-shaded lake has RV hookups and camping facilities available along its south side.

On the north side of the lake, next to K-25, is The Ol' Depot antique store.

As its names implies, the store is housed in the old railroad depot, renovated by the city, and rented to several local antique dealers who decided to put all of their antique eggs in one basket. If you're in the market for antiques at reasonable prices then you had better bring a truck.

Seventy-one miles east of the Kansas-Colorado state line is Decatur County, the only county in Kansas to be named for a naval officer. Stephen Decatur was a hero of the War of 1812 and also battled the pirates of Tripoli in 1815. He is most remembered for saying, "May she always be right; but our country, right or wrong."

Our first stop in Decatur County — and I do hope you'll join me — is Elephant Rock. Six miles from the county line is a sign marking the road to Traer. Take the road north for seven miles, then two miles west to town, then a mile south of town, and Elephant Rock sits atop a hill directly in front of you.

It's an eroded rock formation that, through wind and rain, has transformed into an elephant-shaped natural arch, with eyes. Hence the name. You can easily see the eyes if you have standard 7x35 binoculars. As natural arches go it's not one of the biggies of the world, but try to find another one in Kansas.

Back on U.S. 36 the sign reads "Oberlin, Far More Than You Expect."

Tucked into the valley of Sappa (a Siouan word meaning dark or black) Creek, Oberlin is at the crossroads of U.S. 36 and U.S. 83. From U.S. 36 take Pennsylvania Street south past "Pioneer Family," a Felten sculpture that overlooks the redesigned downtown area. Oberlin also boasts the "World's Greatest Home-owned Fair," held each year in early August.

One of the town's top attractions is the Last Indian Raid Museum. The exhibits highlight early prairie life with a sod house, an 1885 jail and Indian artifacts collected in 1878 from the site of the last Indian raid in Kansas.

More than 40 settlers were killed in northwest Kansas by a band of Cheyenne who fled north from the reservation in Indian Territory, now known as Oklahoma. Several of the area settlers who were killed during the raids are buried in the Oberlin cemetery. A monument in the cemetery commemorates the event.

If August is the month that you choose to travel along U.S. 36 you will notice an abundance of commercial sunflower fields along both sides of the highway. Take the back roads and you'll see the natural version of sunflowers. And for you hunters, there are thousands of mourning doves to take advantage of in September.

On the east edge of Decatur County sits Norcatur, a town name derived from the combination of Norton and Decatur. Norcatur has 226 folks and even though they are few in number they still exhibit great civic spirit by putting up a signing announcing "Norcatur, an Agricultural Community With Pride."

If you like old, Western-style buildings, you ought to take a look at the International Order of Odd Fellows building. It faces east and is worth a visit.

About 12 miles into Norton County is the road south to the Keith Sebelius Reservoir, formerly named Norton Reservoir. It was later renamed in honor of Sen. Keith Sebelius, a politician from western Kansas who served our state for many years in Washington.

At the north shore of the lake is the entrance to Prairie Dog State Park. It not only has camping and boating facilities, it also has an adobe house built in the 1890s, and preserved on its original location. The park is named for the black-tailed prairie dogs that abound in the area. There are many small colonies of the critters within the park boundaries.

The lake is considered by Wildlife and Parks to be one of the top five fishing lakes in Kansas. It is well known for producing record saugeye, wipers up to 20-plus pounds, tons of white crappie and more largemouth bass than you can shake a stick at.

Norton, the town, has a sign that brags "Norton — Where the Best Begins." It was named after Orloff Norton, a captain in the 5th Kansas Cavalry. At the end of South State Street is one of the most colorful football stadiums I have ever seen. It's the home of the Norton Bluejays, and blue is the operative word. If you like to photograph or paint images of old motels then take a look at the U.S. 36 Motel on the south side of the road as you head east out of town.

Norton also has a stagecoach stop, adobe house and the "Also-Ran Gallery of Presidents."

Just into Phillips County is the little town of Prairie View. "A Touch of Dutch" sign welcomes you to this hamlet of 67 Kansans. At least three large and colorful windmills in the yards of homes seem to substantiate the Dutch claim. Prairie is one of the most commonly used names in Kansas. It appears more than 60 times in one fashion or another in Kansas place names.

A place that should not be overlooked is the Dane G. Hansen Memorial Plaza, located in Logan, 11 miles south of Prairie View. It's not often that a small-town boy makes it big at home, then turns around and wills his hometown $15 million. Hansen did just that.

The square-block plaza is the site where Hansen was born, and where he conducted all of his business dealings. To show his appreciation to Logan, and the area, Hansen left the $15 million donation for scholarships, church groups, the Boy Scouts, the construction of community buildings, low-cost housing projects, the Logan Swimming pool and many other community projects.

The Dane G. Museum features a number of fine collections that include European and Western guns, Oriental art, American and foreign coins, and traveling exhibitions from the Smithsonian collection. Hansen's office is part of the exhibit. The museum is free and open to the public.

Back to U.S. 36. At Stuttgart, on the corner of Main and Chicago, sits a limestone sign cut into the shape of Kansas. Its black letters say it plainly: "Stuttgart, Established 1888." More than 100,000 Germans immigrated to Kansas in the late 1800s. Stuttgart is one of the communities where they settled.

Phillips County was named for William Phillips, an abolitionist who was killed by pro-slavers in 1856 when he refused to leave his home in Leavenworth. Phillipsburg, on the other hand, was named for Salina founder William A. Phillips, who was also a reporter for the New York Tribune, a newspaper run by Horace Greeley.

Phillipsburg's sign bills the town as "Market Center of North-Central Kansas." On the northwestern edge of town sits a large oil refinery, the only

one in that part of the state. Downtown in the middle of the business district square is the Phillips County Courthouse. Although Phillipsburg says it is the major market center in north central Kansas, it still has the feel of a small town. It allows shoppers to park in the middle of the street.

Phillipsburg is also the home to the Fort Bissell Museum and, an annual rodeo that attracts wranglers from all across the United States. And at Christmas it becomes the "City of Angels and Lights."

On the eastern edge of Phillips County is Agra. The town's name doesn't have anything to do with local agriculture, but was derived either from Agra, India, the home of the Taj Mahal, or from a local woman.

I've seen some pretty unusual things in my life, but in Agra I saw a long-bearded man wearing a pith helmet. He had two holstered pistols and a rifle in a saddle scabbard. He wasn't riding a horse, though. He was casually peddling his bicycle down the street. I smiled and drove on.

Straight south of Agra is Kirwin Reservoir, another fine fishing hole on the High Plains. Kirwin Reservoir is part of Kirwin National Wildlife Refuge, one of the four NWR in Kansas. The reservoir is well-known for its white and black crappie populations, and an abundance of largemouth bass.

Let's continue east into Smith County, the last county on our northwest Kansas journey.

"Kensington, Near the Birthplace of Home on the Range," the sign says.

Bathed in late-afternoon light, several women gathered around a community bulletin board while two small children played at their feet. A sign stuck in one lawn announced that it was the "Yard of the Month." And so it goes in small town Kansas.

Five miles east of Kensington, right before you get to Athol, take K-8 north for about nine miles to the log cabin where Dr. Brewster Higley wrote the lyrics for "Home on the Range," the Kansas state song.

Higley moved to Smith County from Ohio in the early 1870s. In 1873 his lyrics were first published in the Smith County Pioneer under the title "My Western Home." The music was written a short time later by Dan Kelly, who moved to Kansas in 1872. Both Higley and Kelly left Kansas before 1880.

The route to the cabin is clearly marked. And although the cabin is located on private land it is open to the public 365 days a year. The cabin sits next to a cluster of farmhouses built along the banks of the West Fork of Beaver Creek. It's an idyllic setting and really worth the visit. Culturally, as a Kansan, it's the right thing to do.

Back on U.S. 36 then east to Athol, a name whose origin is shrouded in uncertainty. Historians have listed five possible sources: Athol, N.Y.; Athol, Mass.; Atholl, Scotland; or a railroad official's wife or daughter. You choose whichever sounds best.

"Smith Center, in the Heart of Uncle Sam." Take a drive through the downtown area. There's a fine looking old bank building on the southeast corner; however, the makeshift doorway detracts from the overall beauty of the bank. Swing back up north and stop at Wagner Park. It's a fine place to relax for a picnic or to let the youngsters roam free. The Old Dutch Mill, also in the park, is Smith Center's main historic attraction.

The mill was built by Charles Schwartz between 1879 and 1882. Its timbers were hand-hewn from native logs. The old mill was moved from the Schwartz homestead near Reamsville in southern Smith County to Smith Center in 1938. It is one of two windmills in Kansas. The other is at Wamego in Pottowatomie County.

On to Lebanon, the last official stop on our trip.

In addition to Lebanon being near the center of the 48 contiguous states, it also holds a unique spot in Kansas climatological history. On Feb. 13, 1905, it became the site of the lowest recorded temperature in Kansas history, a minus 40 degrees.

One mile north of town is a stone monument and plaque marking the center of the 48 states. It's off by 1/8-mile because the owner of the land where the exact center is located doesn't want people tromping all over his land. How unKansaslike!

To get back to Wichita I strongly recommend taking K-181 south from Lebanon to Downs, then U.S. 24 to U.S. 81 and south to River City. It's longer but more scenic.

Dotted with grasses and wildflowers, the jagged to the eye but soft to the touch edges of the Arikaree Breaks are highlighted by the early morning light.

A strong statement for preservation

Quivira National Wildlife Refuge is a birder's paradise

When it comes to nature, I think Henry David Thoreau summed it up best when he said, "In wildness lies the preservation of the world." And so it is at Quivira National Wildlife Refuge, where birds and critters roam freely under the protective eye of the U.S. Fish and Wildlife Service.

The 21,800-acre federal refuge is located just east of Hudson in Stafford County. It's open 24 hours a day, 365 days a year, and it doesn't cost you a dime.

Just about any time of year is a good time to visit the refuge, but if you really want to see some diversity in shorebird species then you ought to visit the refuge between April and June, a period when up to 90 percent of the North American shorebird population migrate through the refuge on their way to their spring breeding grounds.

Most Kansans don't realize how important this ancient salt marsh is to migrating shorebirds. If it's a water bird, it comes through Quivira or Cheyenne Bottoms. That's a lot of birds and a lot of species, and your chances of seeing them around your hometown are pretty minimal.

So let's travel to the bird watching mountain, so to speak, to see what we can see.

Take a late April or early May day for example. Before dawn, load up your camera gear and take a leisurely, pre-sunrise drive to Hutchinson, then head west out of Hutch on Fourth Street. It's a pleasant, traffic-free route through the beautiful sandhill country of western Reno County. This straight-as-an-arrow road is bracketed by farmland, cottonwoods and willows.

Keep an eye to the edges of the fields and the road because wildlife moves early and late in the day so your chances of seeing critters are pretty good along this lonely stretch of road. Always have your camera at the ready, just in case.

Twenty-eight miles west of Hutchinson is where you'll turn north for the one-mile drive to the U.S. Fish and Wildlife Service headquarters. Stop in to visit with refuge employees about what they have been seeing on the refuge, and while you're there pick up the free maps and brochures.

Be sure to return to the headquarters after visiting the refuge. The wildlife exhibits are first class and the handicapped accessible trail to the west of the building has a display of interesting birdhouses along the trail. If you like a particular birdhouse the folks at the headquarters have building plans for each.

The map of Quivira is easy to follow, once you orient yourself to the north. Leaving the headquarters, you will drive around the Little Salt Marsh. Both the Big and Little Salt Marsh and all of the smaller ponds are fed by

Rattlesnake Creek, a free-flowing creek that originates near Greensburg.

As I slowly drove by, more than 50 American white pelicans lifted off the Little Salt Marsh and began their single-file rise over the refuge. It's an uncommon sight in Kansas unless you're at Quivira or Cheyenne Bottoms, to the north in Barton County.

Quivira and Cheyenne Bottoms are two large natural sinks that provide life-sustaining feed and rest areas for a number of species of shorebirds as they migrate north from the northern tip of South America to their spring breeding grounds in Canada.

Although the wetlands have traditionally been used and paid for by hunters, these wetlands also provide ample opportunities for wildlife enthusiasts to photograph, sketch or observe the wide variety of species that live in or pass through the refuge.

In an hour I saw more than 200 white pelicans, several American bittern, six broods of Canada geese, dozens of bobwhite quail, several broods of ring-necked pheasants, six black-necked stilts, an immature red-tailed hawk, greater yellowlegs, several black ibis, dowitchers, snowy egrets, cattle egrets, great blue herons, blue-winged teal, wigeon, mallard, swallows, American avocets, killdeer, least terns (an endangered species) and, of course, the ever-popular coot.

And that's just a partial list of the more than 250 species of birds that can be seen at Quivira each year. Every fall Quivira and Cheyenne Bottoms are stopping points for the endangered whooping crane as well as hundreds of thousands of migrating sandhill cranes. The region also draws thousands of bird-watchers who have a positive economic impact on the Stafford County area.

As you round the bend to the west on the north end of the Little Salt Marsh there is a turnout to what was once a prairie dog town. The floods of 1993 wiped out the town and attempts in 1997 to recreate a prairie dog town with critters rounded up in Hutchinson met with another natural disaster of sorts.

Seems that badgers, common to Quivira, love to eat prairie dogs. And the semi-tame prairie dogs from Hutch, lacking in some pretty basic survival skills, quickly fell victim to their natural enemy.

On up the road, keep your eyes open for everything from white-tailed deer to quail. The four coyotes I saw one day all waited long enough for me to take a nice picture of each one. If you stay in your car most of the critters will move away slowly, or watch you as you watch them.

At County Road 484 you can drive west for about 2 1/2 miles to the artesian well. Locals used to fill their jugs with the well water but the practice was stopped recently because of conta-

mination. After leaving the well take the road north and travel three miles, then turn west. Along this road, look to the north and you'll see the nesting grounds of the interior least tern.

This endangered species nests on the salt flats and has a tendency to dive-bomb intruders, with bomb being the operative word. Because least terns are an endangered species, it is against the law to approach the nesting birds. From the road you will see dozens of mounds, built for the nesting terns by refuge personnel. The mounds provide some security during periods of high water but the real danger is from predators like coyotes and bobcats. To keep them at bay the area is surrounded by a low electric fence.

From the salt flats take the wildlife drive to the south. This is a sweet 4 1/2-mile loop past a long pond and the Big Salt Marsh. Take your time as you travel through Quivira. The area abounds with wildlife but you'll miss them if you drive too fast. And always have your camera at the ready.

After visiting Quivira you can make the short drive west to Hudson, the home of Hudson Cream Flour produced at the Stafford County Flour Mills. If you've never been on a tour of a working flour mill, stop by and ask for one. They're available Monday through Thursday.

A rainbow decorates the afternoon sky over the Quivira National Wildlife Refuge.

A flight of white pelicans takes to the air at Quivira National Wildlife Refuge in Stafford County.

For area information:

Quivira National Wildlife Refuge, Refuge Manager Dave Hilley, Route 3, Box 48A, Stafford, Kan. 67578 or call (316) 486-2393.

Cheyenne Bottoms Waterfowl Management Area, Area Manager Karl Grover, Route 3, Box 301, Great Bend, Kan. 67530 or call (316) 793-7730.

Stafford County Flour Mills, Hudson, Kan. (316) 458-4121.

Reno: One really big county

State fair aside, Reno County has a lot to offer

Each year the folks in Reno County throw a whopper of a party at Hutchinson. Dress is casual and the food — Pronto Pups, saltwater taffy, funnel cakes — is served in copious amounts. The occasion is the Kansas State Fair each September on the fairgrounds at the north end of Hutchinson. Be there.

A little history. Established in 1867, the 1,259 square mile county was named after Gen. Jesse Lee Reno, a West Point graduate. In 1862 Reno literally was shot out of his saddle at South Mountain, Md., by Confederate troops whom Reno believed had left the area. Several troops under Reno's command were Kansans, and when they returned from the war they decided to name a county in honor of their late commander.

Since you're all going to be in Reno County anyway you might just as well travel around a bit before, during or after your visit to the fairgrounds. Reno County is a pretty sizable chunk of land, so I'll just dance around the landscape some and you can cut in anywhere.

Some river stuff. By the time the Arkansas River has entered the county north of Nickerson it has become a wide and attractive body of water. Abundant wildlife along the river's edge make it a good idea to slow down and be alert to the many photographic possibilities during the 26 or so miles the river traverses before leaving the county southeast of Haven.

The Arkansas is one of the three public rivers in Kansas, which means once you gain access to the water you can take the river all the way to the Gulf of Mexico if you want. The other two rivers are the Kansas River from Junction City to its confluence with the Missouri River, which is the third public waterway.

In the southeast corner of the county are the friendly little town of St. Joe and Cheney Reservoir, a 9,500-acre impoundment fed by the North Fork of the Ninnescah River. Cheney State Park is one of the top three most visited parks in Kansas.

If you're traveling into Reno County from Wichita you'll pass Yoder on K-96, the center of Amish culture in Kansas. When Eli Yoder came to Kansas from Pennsylvania in the 1880s I doubt he envisioned his town to be the attraction it is today. The Dutch Mill bakery, which whips up great sweet rolls and breads Monday through Saturday, and the horse-drawn buggies hitched up at the hardware store are two of the more popular attractions in town.

On down K-96 is Haven, another one of those towns you pass by on your way to Hutchinson. Stop in and visit the downtown and residential areas. If you enjoy church architecture take the Arlington road west out of town and stop by St. Paul Lutheran Church, a half-mile mile west of Haven.

West and south of Haven is Castleton, the Kansas namesake of Castleton, Vt. The economy of Castleton has been pretty well whittled away by time and events, but the town is still home to a number of families. At the front of a small park sits a marble memorial honoring the Castleton men who served in World War II. It was erected on Veterans Day in 1950 and specifically honors Dwight Van Hoozen and Vern Gibb; both died during World War II.

During my last visit to Castletown there were two churches on the west end of town pretty much end to end: The Castleton Union Community Church and St. Agnes Catholic Church. Next to St. Agnes was a playhouse-size version of the larger building.

Eight miles to the southwest is Pretty Prairie. It's home to Kansas' largest night rodeo, held each year in July. Town records show that Mary Collingwood and her nine children moved to Pretty Prairie from Indiana in 1872. When they broke ground the following spring she made note of how pretty the prairie was. The rest is history.

West on the county blacktop is Lerado. I'm sorry to say Lerado is pretty much dust in the winds of time

Attractive murals like the one gracing the side of a restaurant in Arlington are becoming commonplace throughout Kansas.

The Cosmosphere in Hutchinson is one of Reno County's most popular tourist attractions. The Cosmosphere is located at the south edge of the campus of Hutchinson Community College.

except for the Lerado Community Church, a community building, and the cemetery north of where the town once stood.

The town had its genesis in 1884 when its founder, John Brady, heard strong rumors that the Rock Island and Missouri Pacific railroads would be building lines that would cross each other on their respective routes from Hutchinson to the southwest and Kingman to the northwest. In that era a town built on the junction of two railroads was sure to be a hub of commerce.

Brady, a wealthy man, could not pass up an opportunity to build a town where the lines were sure to cross. He built a two-story bank, and in no time other businesses followed — a livery stable, harness shop, barber shop, the offices of two doctors and the Indiana Cafe with a sign that boasted, "Meals at all hours and oysters in season."

As expected, both railroads sent surveyors through the small but growing town. The Rock Island demanded free land for right of way and switchyards. Brady agreed but balked when the railroad company also demanded 51 percent of the town company's holdings. Brady, certain that the railroads would give in, refused to negotiate.

Both railroads routed their lines through Turon and Penalosa. By 1887, Brady, his empire dwindling along with his cash, moved back to his home in Kentucky. The boom in Lerado lasted for three years then steadily declined.

One interesting note is the name. Originally called Leredo for the town in Texas, the second "e" was accidentally changed to an "a" through a clerical error at the post office department in Washington.

West and north to Turon, the town of several names. You can call it Cottonwood Grove or Pioneer City, two early names, but Turon is what was settled on in honor of the Italian city of Turin. Why the spelling change? Stop there and ask.

At Turon you can travel north to Sylvia, named in 1887 for the wife and daughter of Albert Robinson, an official with the St. Joseph and Denver City Railroad. At Sylvia get on U.S. 50 to Hutchinson, or you can take K-61 east to Langdon.

At Langdon, named for a store owner whose first name escapes everyone, you'll find several rustic old storefronts on the main street. One block to the west is an interesting silver building that was once a movie house. It presents some stark textural possibilities for photographs or drawings at just about any time of day.

Entering Arlington on K-61 is a nice twist-and-turn departure from most straight drives through small towns. Arlington, named for Arlington Heights, Mass., has a main street that runs from the heights on the west side of town through the business district. There are two restaurants to choose from if you're interested in a good lunch or supper.

From Arlington take K-14 north to Abbyville. In 1866 the founders of this small town decided to name their town after Abby McLean, the first child born there. On the edge of town is a street named Abby.

From Abbyville avoid U.S. 50 by taking the blacktop (old U.S. 50) to Plevna. At Plevna you'll find a tidy little town with an interesting history and remains of what was once the Plevna General Store. The store burned to the ground several years ago.

The town took its name from Plevna, Bulgaria, where in 1877 the Russians and Turks battled for several months in what was called the Breakfast War. It was the first war in which correspondents had unlimited access. That access allowed newspaper subscribers in the Western world to read about the war at the breakfast table each day.

From Plevna travel east through Abbyville to Partridge. Originally known as Reno Centre, Partridge was later renamed for the maiden name of a railroad official's wife.

Just east of where K-61 and U.S. 50 intersect is Whiteside, where you'll find the well-known Dutch Kitchen Restaurant and Stutzman Greenhouse. Both places provide visitors a nice combination of ingredients — that is to say you can eat and buy your greens within 50 yards of each other.

On to the east is South Hutchinson, a thriving community with its own city government and police department. Incorporated in 1887, South Hutchinson came into existence in part because of a false rumor that oil had been discovered across the Arkansas River south of Hutchinson.

It was a ruse turned ugly when the landowners who perpetrated the rumor found out that the people who had bought the land were digging up large deposits of salt, not oil. Salt is king in these parts, and a few would-be oil barons became salt barons instead. In the bargain South Hutchinson became a town.

Take the main drag north through South Hutchinson which eventually turns into the Woodie Seat Freeway, what must be Kansas' shortest freeway. Seat, former mayor of Hutchinson, died in a car crash. The very short, four-lane freeway was named in his honor.

The Ken Kennedy Expressway on K-61 from Carey Park to the northern city limits was named in honor of Kennedy, a Hutchinson police officer killed in the line of duty during a stakeout.

Hutchinson has much to offer. Visitors would do well to start at the Reno County Museum at A and Walnut streets. Visit the permanent exhibit "Reno County: The First Fifty Years" and you'll get a good look at each town in the county through individual town exhibits. Reno Countians should be very proud of their museum; it's a first-class facility, and it continues to expand. Admission is free. If you have questions, call (316) 662-1184.

The crown jewel for visitors to Hutchinson is the Kansas Cosmosphere and Space Center at 1100 N. Plum, just south of Hutchinson Community College. The facility features the Hall of Space, Planetarium, an original SR-71, and the awesome Omnimax, a big-as-life projection system.

Additionally, the Teachers and Space and Future Astronaut training programs provide teachers and students a hands-on look at space and space exploration. The Kansas Cosmosphere and Space Center is considered one of the finest repositories of space travel history in the United States. For information about instructional programs and Omnimax showings, call (316) 662-2305.

If you're looking for a place to sit a spell then drive south on Main Street to Carey Park. It's a big park with an excellent new zoo in the southeast part, an 18-hole public golf course, a disc golf course, picnic facilities and some really nice walkways for an evening stroll.

Another fine natural setting is the Dillon Nature Center and Lake. The Center has hiking trails, canoeing, fishing and educational programs. It's east on 30th Street past K-61; call (316) 663-7411 for more information.

Just up the road from the Dillon Nature Center is Sand Hill State Park. The park has more than 2 miles of hiking trails and offers limited hunting during the fall.

North of Hutchinson on K-96 is the small community of Willowbrook. It is, by income definition in 1989, the community with the highest per capita income in Kansas. Founded in the 1920s by the Carey Salt family, it is the epitome of country squire living, complete with a golf course and curving drives. It's surrounded by a levy to keep out Cow Creek.

Visitors are guided into the community between two large white brick pillars that straddle the entryway. While driving through this tree-canopied plantation atmosphere I could swear I heard the strains of George and Ira Gershwin's "Summertime".

Farther north on K-96 is Nickerson, where the camels and ostriches play. The Hedricks Exotic Animal Farm sits on the south edge of town, and the sight of three or four camels mucking about in the mud or an ostrich cruising a fence line is quite an eye opener when you're not expecting it.

East of Nickerson is Medora, primarily a bedroom community for Hutchinson. In the past Medora was crow capital of Kansas from November through February. Wichita now holds that distinction.

Our final Reno County stop is Buhler. Entering town from the west you'll see a large used-combine lot on the edge of town. If you've ever wondered where combines go to die you can stop wondering — they go to Buhler.

All kidding aside, Buhler is an attractive community with a wide main street and, as small towns go, a coordinated look to the downtown business architecture. The attractive city park on the east side of town sports a fishing pond for youngsters and retirees, a swimming pool and good picnic facilities.

A monument describing President Warren G. Harding's visit to Kansas sits next to the county road (4th Street) leading west out of Hutchinson. Harding, perhaps America's most controversial president, drove a combine in a field next to where the monument is located.

Sprays of bright yellow sunflowers line Kansas roadways each September.

A Visit to the Smoky Hills

From oil to rocks to Roller Coaster Road, Russell County wears its beauty well

Russell County, located in the north-central part of our state is an excellent day trip, and it's an easy drive from almost anywhere in the state. Keeping that in mind, let's take an up-close look at the valleys of the Saline and Smoky Hill rivers. From Wichita take I-135 north to I-70, then west to Dorrance, our first stop, just inside Russell County.

The folks in Dorrance like to hoop it up, if you'll pardon the pun. On the west edge of town is Pro Bound Sports, the makers of basketball supports used at high schools and colleges throughout the Great Plains.

If you would like a tour of the plant call Heddy Mahoney at (785) 666-4207. And since you're there, ask the folks at the plant about interesting, out-of-the-way places to visit during your tour of Russell County. You'll like Dorrance.

The people are friendly and the downtown is photogenic, particularly in the early morning or evening. Dorrance was named after either O.B. Dorrance, superintendent of the Kansas Pacific Railroad, or Dorrance, N.H.

Now for some back-road travel.

From I-70 take the blacktop straight north from Dorrance for three miles, then left (west) at the corral on the northwest corner for a pleasant drive to Bunker Hill.

Locally it's known as the lakeshore road. We'll be taking a portion of this road, but if you see another road on the DeLorme map that looks good feel free to get to Bunker Hill any way you wish.

It's easy to see why they call this post rock country. When settlers first moved to Russell County in the late 1800s they found few trees but plenty of limestone. It followed that if fences and houses were to be constructed then limestone would be the building material.

This part of the lakeshore road, as with most of the county roads in the Smoky Hills, is lined with aging but sturdy stone posts that will serve their owners far into the next century. To the north you'll catch occasional glimpses of Wilson Reservoir. We'll visit there later.

Bunker Hill has several attractive, turn-of-the-century buildings in the downtown area. Two of those buildings face each other and both are worth a visit. Smoky Hills Public TV, otherwise known as KOOD, is housed in the circa-1887 redbrick structure with limestone trim.

Across the street is the 1916 structure that houses the Bunker Hill Cafe. For the past 25 years Tom and Janet Taggart have run this well-known eatery, which attracts patrons from all over Kansas. Particularly notable are the steaks, catfish and raisin bread served Wednesday through Saturday from 5 to 10 p.m. Their telephone number is (785) 483-6544.

At the corner of Sixth and Elm is a small park with a sheltered picnic area and playground equipment. One block east of there is the Bunker Hill museum, dedicated to Mary A. "Mother" Bickerdyke, Civil War nurse. It's open Sundays and holidays from 1:30 to 5 p.m.

Russell, originally known as Fossil Station in 1867, is the county seat and an oil town. Evidence of its "black gold" past and present is everywhere you look. Pump jacks, portable rigs, wire rope vendors, storage tanks and a plethora of oil-related industries are scattered throughout town.

There are several museums in town. The Oil Patch Museum near I-70 and the Fossil Station Museum near downtown are open Memorial Day through Labor Day. The Gernon House, a block east of the primary north-south street, was the first stone home built in the county and the home of Russell's first blacksmith.

The Fossil Station Museum is an unusual limestone building that serves, more or less, as the Russell County historical museum. It has displays depicting the county's railroad, post rock, oil, cattle and settler history.

Russell has several attractive buildings, including the county courthouse, the high school, and a number of homes and museums. At the east entrance of town on U.S. 40 is a historical marker that tells about one of the last battles in Kansas between the Indians and white men.

The Cheyenne, Arapaho and other Plains Indians became increasingly concerned about Kansas Pacific Railroad workers disturbing their hunting grounds. In May 1869 a band of Indians attacked seven railroaders who were working on the track near where Russell stands today. The workers jumped on a handcar and pumped furiously toward their camp. Two workers were shot dead off the car, and four more were wounded. A memorial to the dead can be found in the cemetery on the east side of town near the marker.

For additional information on Russell, call the Chamber of Commerce at (785) 483-6960 or visit their office at 610 N. Main.

A close look at the map revealed only one Russell County town below I-70. Not wanting to overlook any possibility, I headed for Milberger. What I found is pretty much just a crossroads. From Milberger travel six miles west on a county road and then 12 miles north to Gorham, the home of St. Mary's Catholic Church.

Although I'm not much of a churchgoer, I do love to visit churches, and St. Mary's is a wonderful example of the limestone churches that dot the Russell-Ellis County area. The stenciling inside is simple and beautiful. You ought to drop by for a visit; the doors are always open.

From Gorham take old U.S. 40 back to Russell, get on the main north-south street and drive north to 15th Street. Turn west at 15th and drive to the edge of town. From the west edge of town drive for about 1 3/4 miles until the road curves to your right (north) down a hill.

You are now on Canyon Road, or the road to Paradise. From there drive seven twisting-turning miles north to a four-way intersection. At the stop sign turn right, go about a block, then take the road north. I don't know the local name for this stretch of bedrock, but I call it Roller Coaster Road and defy anyone to give it a better name. For five miles you'll drive up and down a quick succession of hills and valleys that eventually drop you into the valley of Paradise Creek and the town of Paradise.

When Wichita founder J.R. Mead and the members of his hunting party came to this area in the 1800s, he looked around at all of the game and the beautiful valley and said, "This must be Paradise," and so it is. On the hill overlooking town from the north is the only limestone water tower I've ever seen.

East from Paradise on U.S. 281 is Waldo. Stop there and visit what's left of an original log cabin in what's left of a park in what's left of downtown Waldo. Don't get the wrong idea, though. There are a number of families that still call Waldo home.

The Fossil Station Museum in Russell is an attractive warehouse of Russell County historical icons and information.

Further east is a small but prosperous town with a colorful sign: "Welcome to Luray — Halfway between Paradise and the Garden of Eden." On the north edge of Luray is the city park where the first log cabin in Russell County was built.

If you think small towns are dying then you had better look again because Luray isn't paying any attention to demographics. New curbs, the Rambling Rose restaurant and the stately, redecorated building that houses the senior center are just a few of the indicators that this small town of 295 folks is alive and well.

If you haven't been to the Garden of Eden at Lucas then you've missed an important part of America's folk art history. There isn't enough space here to accurately describe just how unusual S.P. Dinsmoor was, and continues to be, through his legacy in concrete and limestone.

Dinsmoor was a Civil War veteran who, after his first wife died, married an attractive 20-year-old woman when he was 80. He then fathered a son and daughter, both of whom are still living. Dinsmoor was in the Civil War, his son was in Vietnam. Think about that for a second.

Suffice it to say that you would be remiss to not stop at the Garden of Eden to tour this incredible monument to one man's commitment to art, poli-

tics and just plain hard work. It's open daily 10 a.m. to 5 p.m. from April through November. The $4 admission is worth the price. Kids under 12 are free. For more information, call (785) 525-6395.

Brant's Meat Market is an excellent place to visit in downtown Lucas. George and Doug Brant, father and son, have been making fine homemade sausages, bologna and jaternice (it-er-nit-c) for decades. They're open Monday to Friday from 7:30 a.m. to 5:30 p.m. and Saturday from 7:30 a.m. to 10 p.m. Lucas merchants have a longtime tradition of staying open on Saturday night until 10.

Also downtown is a small but well-appointed park and the new home/museum of the Kansas Grass Roots Art Association. On permanent display are the works of Inez Marshall, a sculptress from Portis who in her lifetime created whimsical creations from limestone. The Marshall collection was broken up after her death but thanks to the efforts of the KGRAA the bulk of her work was collected for display in Lucas.

The museum also displays the work of other folk artists from Kansas and other parts of the country. The museum as well as a number of the civic improvement projects in Lucas were funded with grants in excess of $200,000. Not bad for an out of the way town in the Smoky Hills.

Straight south from Lucas is picturesque Wilson Reservoir, filled with 9,000 acres of the coolest, cleanest and almost deepest water in Kansas. Wilson's 14,000 acres of state and federally managed land offer excellent camping and picnicking facilities in five parks. Other attractions include the Burr Oak Nature Trail for hikers (accessible to the handicapped), the David Mullins Archery Range, three swimming beaches, the Rocktown Nature Area and a marina for boaters.

When the wind is right you can watch turkey vultures or birds of prey hover over the face of the dam as they search for an easy meal below. Wilson Reservoir, considered by many anglers as one of the finest fisheries in Kansas, consistently holds the records for smallmouth bass, walleye and stripers.

The reservoir and surrounding area is a beautiful slice of the Smoky Hills, a place where you should kick back in one of the many excellent camping areas and enjoy an unbelievably fine sunset. For information about federal facilities at the lake, call the Army Corps of Engineers at (785) 658-2551 or the Wildlife and Parks Department at (785) 658-2465.

Adding new meaning to "special"

Stafford County glows with down-home friendliness

There's something special about Stafford County.

Perhaps it's the way the beautiful sand hills nestle up to everything, or maybe it's the abundance of wildlife and wildflowers. Whatever its special qualities are, I'm certain you'll recognize them the moment you arrive in this south central Kansas county.

As I drove into the county, two fawns, their spots fading into adulthood, sprang from their hiding place in a locust grove as I neared Neola in southeast Stafford County. As the fawns escaped into the soft, flowing landscape they flushed up a dozen mourning doves and an American kestrel from the same grove. A little farther down the road five young wild turkeys fed along the edge of the road. So it goes on a morning drive to Neola.

To get there from Wichita take U.S. 54 to Cunningham, then take the paved road north to Turon where you pick up the blacktop straight west to the first blacktop north. Go north for two to three miles and you'll cross a railroad track. Take the next blacktop west and presto, you're in Neola.

The town itself is little more than a grain elevator and one house, but there continues to be a minor dispute about how the town was named. A diary kept by a woman who helped settle Neola indicates that settlers from Neola, Iowa, named the place.

Another, more colorful, story says that a local man by the name of Eli named the town after Neola, his favorite milk cow. You choose the story you like best but I'm partial to the one about the milk cow.

To the north of Neola is Zenith. The businesses are gone save the stark white co-op elevator and the Zenith Community Church which at one time advertised itself as being "prayer conditioned."

In what was the downtown area sits a sturdy redbrick building with a corrugated metal awning. Once a bank, it is in the process of being repossessed by nature, the ultimate lien holder. The bank and the rest of Zenith's crumbling business district are slowly but surely disappearing beneath an onslaught of trees, shrubs and time.

West on U.S. 50 is Stafford, the namesake town of the county, but not the county seat. Stafford County is one of many Kansas counties named for Civil War veterans. Established in 1867, it was named in honor of Capt. Lewis Stafford who served with the 1st Kansas Infantry. Stafford was, for a time, incarcerated in the infamous Andersonville prison and eventually died at the Battle of Young's Point in Louisiana.

As in most Kansas towns, the people in Stafford are friendly, always taking the time to wave or say hello to a stranger. Downtown at Main and Broadway is the Stafford County museum, open Monday through Thursday from 1:30 to 3:30 p.m. and Saturday and Sunday from 2 to 4 p.m.

The Stafford High School at Park and Broadway is an attractive, three-story brick building that continues to serve the community. Many of Stafford's streets are also brick. A drive around any small town will reveal a number of interesting architectural ideas that might fit nicely into your building or restoration plans. Keep your camera handy to document some of the nice gingerbread trim, porches and brickwork.

The city library is an attractive building with beveled glass windows, fine woodwork and a large and beautiful stained-glass window portrait. The building was "Erected in Loving memory of Nora Emily Larabee by her Father and Mother." Call ahead — (316) 234-5762 — to ensure that the library is open when you visit Stafford; it's worth the extra effort.

The Stafford County Historical and Genealogical Society and Museum is located at 100 S. Main. The museum is filled with images, artwork and historical pieces reflecting the history of Stafford County.

Driving west on Broadway will take you out of town on the old version of U.S. 50. There's substantially less traffic here than on the newer version. A few miles out you'll pass the Stafford airport with its two well-kept grass runways. Another two miles or so and you'll come to a "Y" in the road where a decision about being normal or adventurous will have to be made.

The road left (south) takes you back to the new U.S. 50; the road right (north) is another story. If you turn right travel for about one-half mile, then take the first left (west) and you'll be on the back road to Dillwyn and Macksville.

The road is vintage sand hills, soft and occasionally bumpy. It will give you an up-close-and-personal look at the natural beauty of this rolling, wildflower and tree-lined landscape. You may think I have put you on the road to oblivion, but it's a good road and will take you to a paved highway in just six beautiful miles.

About four miles into the six you'll cross the paved road that travels north to St. John; ignore it. After a few more miles of sand road you'll hit a paved road that will attempt to take you back to new U.S. 50. When the paved road curves south go straight ahead on the sand road to Dillwyn.

Dillwyn is no more than a two-story gray house, a grain elevator and a one-story yellow house to the west. Ignore the paved road back to U.S. 50 and follow the sand road past and in between the grain elevators to Macksville.

If you've stayed on back roads all the way you should arrive on the north end of the main street next to Macksville International Airport (okay, maybe just Macksville airport). The runway is a dizzying 2,000 feet above sea level.

Drive south along the main street toward U.S. 50 and take in the well-kept downtown area. Named for its first postmaster, Macksville came into being in 1879 and with a population of 499 it continues to hold its own in modern, move-out-of-the-country times.

On the highway is a place you ought to stop by for lunch. It's called Edna's Place — "Home of Nancy's Big Mama." Nancy Olmsted bought the place from Edna Wood more than a decade ago and continues to make her famous "Big Mama" half-pound hamburger and fries.

The hand-lettered sign outside isn't fancy, but inside you'll find a comfortable, L-shaped lunch counter with seating for seven and two booths against the east wall. Wherever I travel in Kansas, I always try the chicken-fried steak, and the one at Edna's was mighty good.

For less than $4 I got the steak, mashed potatoes, gravy, green beans, a dinner roll and peaches for dessert. If all the cars and pickup trucks are any indication of a good place to eat, then Edna's is the hot spot on U.S. 50 in Stafford County.

One block east of the main street is the Macksville city park. The folks in Macksville care a great deal about their park. It's landscaped in gently rolling hills for youngsters to roll down and has well-manicured brick walkways for a morning or evening stroll. Two bridges, one brick and one stone, span a small manmade canal. A beautiful sandstone band shell facing a landscaped amphitheater on the southeast corner, plenty of picnic tables and a clean playground make this a very fine park.

Big humor in a small package takes form in an epitaph for a dog that strayed into a well-groomed yard in Stafford.

There are several ways to get to St. John, the Stafford County seat. You choose the one that suits you best.

Named for Kansas Gov. John P. St. John, it is one of those wonderful Kansas towns built on a town square and surrounded by the business district. Across the street from the southeast corner of the square is the beautiful county courthouse, circa 1929 art deco style.

If you like this period in architecture then you'll love this wonderful structure. The elevator inside is unusual because it has windows on either side to look out when going up or down. There are many other things to see in St. John, so take your time. When you're through, drive north on U.S. 281 to Seward and Radium.

On the road north you'll cross over Rattlesnake Creek, the main source of water for Quivira National Wildlife Refuge. Just past mile marker 82 is a county road east. This is a good, straight-as-an-arrow drive to Hutchinson. It also skirts the southern edge of the 21,000-acre Quivira National Wildlife Refuge.

When you reach K-l9 turn left (west) for a short drive to Seward, named for William H. Seward, President Lincoln's secretary of state. In Seward are St. Xavier's Catholic Church, a post office and city hall housed in an old school building, and J&J's Cafe, available for your dining pleasure.

The cafe is housed in something a little out of the ordinary: a mobile home.

Sparkling clean with a small lunch counter and plenty of tables, the cafe is open every day but Monday. Stop by and visit.

West is Radium. The school is closed, but Radium continues to be home to a number of folks who work elsewhere but prefer the county feel of a small town.

On the north end of Radium is a friendly pub called the Filling Station. It sits across the street from the co-op and has the feel of an excellent place to have a bottle of pop and shoot the breeze.

I even ran into a childhood friend from my neighborhood in Newton. When Bill Berryman walked in and said, "Steve Harper, what the hell are you doing in Radium, Kansas?" I said, "Having a good time, Bill."

Trekking beyond the obvious

Some of Topeka's finest treasures are off the beaten path

It's hard to imagine that our state Capitol was built for the paltry sum of $3,200,588.92, especially when you consider the amount of hardwoods, brass and copper and the tons of beautifully sculpted marble that went into the interior.

Heck, these days you couldn't even get a decent-size office building for that kind of money. And you sure wouldn't get any fancy furnishings. Oh, maybe a couple of hardwood doors, but nothing to write home about.

Any time is a good time to visit your Capitol building, but the summer is prime time because the place is pretty much empty. Not that there isn't a lot going on, but when the Legislature isn't in session and schoolchildren by the busload aren't touring, then the pace slows considerably, allowing you to take a more leisurely, instructional stroll through this fine building.

You can tour the building on your own or you can hook up with the folks at the first-floor Tourist Information Center in the middle of the rotunda and take one of their excellent tours. The guides work for the state's travel and tourism division and really know their stuff.

It might be kind of fun to bone up on the history of the building before you visit and see if you can stump your guide with a good question. I strongly recommend the guided tours because you can learn a lot more from the guides than you can by aimlessly wandering the halls.

The high point of the tour, so to speak, is where it begins — at the base of the dome. This is the spooky part. You must be 18 or accompanied by an adult and you must sign a release before ascending the stairway to the glass area within the dome you see from outside.

The distance from the information booth to the top of the dome is 304 feet, only a few feet shorter than the Capitol in Washington, D.C.

Tour guides stopped taking visitors to the top of the dome years ago because of the danger. That dizzying part of the trip is for the none-but-the-brave crowd.

From the dome, you will visit the fifth floor for a fine view of the four upper-dome murals. Kansas seems a state destined to be involved in morality issues, and these murals are early remnants of one of those disputes.

History has it that the ruling Populist Party of 1898 commissioned Jerome Fedeli, an Italian artist, to paint the panels. Fedeli's paintings included several half-naked Grecian women, which greatly offended the Republicans.

When the Republicans came to power in 1902, they promptly hired artists from the Chicago firm of Crossman and Study to paint something more dignified and appropriate for Kansans to view.

The four murals depict the themes of knowledge, power, plenty and peace. In 1978 an artist from Arkansas was commissioned to restore several murals that had been water-damaged because of a leaky ceiling.

During the restoration, he added his own bit of immortality to the works by painting his self-portrait in the west panel. If you look closely at the woman holding the painting you'll see the artist's face on her canvas.

The fourth floor is used primarily for legislative offices and is decked out with black-and-white Georgian marble wainscoting and floors. The doors and frames are of sturdy oak.

The House of Representatives and Senate chambers are on the third floor, with the rotunda separating the two. Around the rotunda is a large brass railing where lobbyists wait to peddle their point of view to our representatives. A lot of wheeling and dealing has been done around that railing.

I'll leave the interesting details of the House and Senate chambers to the guides because they present them so well. But I'll tell you that the Senate's ceiling was done by Egyptians, the desks are Kansas cherry wood, and if you look real close, there are two faces in the marble walls of the Senate.

These stately halls definitely were not built by the low bidder. If you like big, powerful art then you'll enjoy the most prominent image on the second floor,

John Steuart Curry's rendition of John Brown and the violent conflicts pitting brother against brother during the Civil War. It is a powerful, captivating image.

Controversy swirled around Curry as he painted this magnificent mural. Many of his detractors said that Brown was not representative of Kansas because he lived here only a short time. But the artist would not buckle to criticism.

Curry's problems didn't stop with the John Brown mural. He originally planned to paint a continuous mural from the east wing to the west wing connected by murals through the rotunda area. He wanted the murals to be the same height, but that would have required the removal of marble wainscoting and state officials would have none of that. Curry died in 1946 before the controversy was resolved.

The rotunda murals were later painted by Lumen Martin Winter of Santa Fe, N.M. Martin, a native of Belpre, finished and installed the paintings in 1978, and is depicted in two of his works. He's the little boy watching the tornado while his classmates run to a storm shelter, and the boy carrying water buckets to the fields in the threshing work.

The most recent artworks installed in the rotunda are on the second floor. Four 8-foot limestone statues of President Dwight Eisenhower, aviatrix Amelia Earhart, publisher William Allen

White and U.S. Sen. Arthur Capper were sculpted by noted Kansas artist Peter Felten of Hays. They were installed in 1982.

These are just a few of the bits and pieces of Kansas history that the tour guides will tell you about on their hour-long tours. If your group is small enough, they will answer as many questions as possible. To schedule a Capitol tour, call (785) 296-3966. Admission is free, and the tours are given Monday through Saturday, 8 a.m. to 4 p.m.

Another exceptional yet virtually unknown free attraction in Topeka is the Kansas Museum of History at 6425 Southwest Sixth Street. It's one of those wonderful places that locals know about and visit but often is overlooked by the casual day-tripper.

Dedicated in 1984, this striking building is not just a willy-nilly repository of what was, but a well-conceived, informative and thoughtful presentation of Kansas' rich history and artifacts.

As a visitor, you get a fine sense of light and space when you enter the building. The highly polished parquet floor is a reflection of the high quality of the exhibits. This is no cheaply furnished place, yet it costs nothing to visit.

On your left is a visitor information area with plenty of brochures and a member of the museum staff to answer your questions. A gift shop full of Kansas memorabilia, books and trinkets

Located in the rotunda is one of the state capitol's four murals depicting knowledge, power, plenty and peace. In 1978 an artist from Arkansas was hired to restore several of the murals. Wanting to add his visage to Kansas history he painted his own image on the tablet held by the woman on the right.

A state capitol guide shows the murals to a group of schoolchildren. Tours are very much a part of everyday life in the capitol building.

is to your right, and a snack area is available when you feel the need for a break.

Now that you are oriented, it is time for a first-class course in Kansas history as you begin your odyssey in the main gallery.

The permanent exhibit "Voices From the Heartland: A Kansas Legacy" begins with our first settlers, the Paleo-Indians who lived in Kansas around 12,000 B.C. Spear points, clay pots and other artifacts are featured as you walk past the life-size and historically accurate replicas of a grass lodge used by the Wichita Indians, a teepee and a buffalo wallow complete with the sounds of the prairie.

Then comes a depiction of the white man in his freight wagons and prairie schooners as the display brings us to 1854, when Kansas became a territory.

The second area, "Ad Astra Per Aspera," deals with those unruly times from 1854 through 1865, when Kansas struggled from territory to statehood.

In the "Bloody Kansas" exhibit, slavery and the Civil War are presented in a series of displays featuring documents, photographs, artifacts and weapons from that era. The well-researched displays bring history alive in ways that are especially interesting for students who find it difficult to put a name or face on important historical events.

"The Twentieth Century" area is something to behold. This section is dedicated to interpreting our recent past, no easy task in a world that continues to speed up at an alarming rate. As you round the corner into the exhibit, you'll see suspended from the ceiling the first aircraft built and flown in Kansas. The owner, builder and pilot was A.K. Longren of Topeka. Below it is a Chevy Eagle automobile that sold for the princely sum of $565 in 1933.

And then there's the Cyrus K. Holliday locomotive, tender and two cars. Yes, a full-sized steam locomotive with wonderful interpretative displays to look at on one side and a completely restored drovers' car and railway executive car on the other side. I'm telling you, this is a big building with a lot of room to grow.

"Our Recent Past" is a lively look at the 1940s through the '80s. As a child of the '40s, I find it particularly interesting to watch and listen to an 18-minute videotape presentation by former Kansan Bill Kurtis. The tape is full of old footage that highlights the multitude of significant events since 1940. It is a fast-paced visual, full of sounds that remind us of where we've been, while bringing us up to date on where we are. Popular tunes from our recent past bring back a flood of memories: Do you remember where you were when you first heard "Boogie Woogie Bugle Boy"?

Topping off the "Our Recent Past" exhibit is "Dorothy's Rainbow Diner." The walk-in diner, complete with polished stainless steel trim, will delight even the most stoic visitor. On the counter is a videotape presentation that will knock your socks off as Dorothy and the folks at her diner talk to you about food and nutrition.

Dorothy talks to you through touch-screen television. Touch the screen and you are able to call up menus for breakfast, daily specials, soups and sides, drinks, short orders and desserts.

Touch the screen again to make your selection and Dorothy pops back with your food and tells you about the nutritional value of that item.

To the right of the entrance is an area designed for youngsters, "From Gems to Gimcracks: The Discovery Place." Folks of all ages will have a big time learning about history through hands-on experiences with a variety of touchable artifacts. Children can get a better feel for history by dressing in clothes from a variety of time periods and cultural backgrounds.

For more information on the programs the museum has to offer, contact the Kansas Museum of History, 6425 S.W. Sixth St., Topeka, KS 66615-1099 or call (785) 272-8681.

Other Topeka attractions are Cedar Crest Governor's Mansion tours at Fairlawn and Cedar Crest streets, the Combat Air Museum at Forbes Field on the south edge of Topeka, Lake Shawnee, the Menninger Foundation

Museum near the museum of history, Mulvane Art Center on the campus of Washburn University, the Topeka Zoo and Reinisch Rose Garden in Gage Park, Sixth and Gage, and the Ward-Meade Home, Ward-Meade Park, 124 N.W. Fillmore.

For more tourist information, call the Kansas division of Travel and Tourism at (800) 252-6727.

Did You Know?

Which president was a Kansan?
Dwight Eisenhower, the 34th president of the 34th state

Where was the first electric street light installed in Wichita?
Douglas and Topeka

What were "Beecher's Bibles"?
Rifles

What was the first railroad built across Kansas east to west?
Kansas Pacific, now Union Pacific

When was Kansas Territory opened to settlement by an act of Congress?
May 20, 1854

What was the name of William Allen White's home in Emporia?
Red Rocks

What frontiersman was sent to Kansas to teach white agriculture to the Kansas Indians?
Daniel Boone

What's Kansas' longest river?
Arkansas

Why did Carry Nation leave her first husband?
Because of his alcoholism

Where is the annual Pancake Race held on Shrove Tuesday?
Liberal in Seward County

When the Santa Fe railroad rebuilt its road into the extinct town of Gerlane, what did it use to make the fill in 1924?
Rock quarried from New Mexico beds containing gold valued at $3 a ton. It was too expensive to mine.

What was the first university to open in Kansas?
Highland University in Doniphan County, 1858

In what city was Kansas Day born in 1877?
Paola in Miami County

Which entertainer on the "Carol Burnett Show" was born in Kansas City, Kan., in 1935?
Lyle Waggoner

Kansas Bait, made in 1913, and developed by Kansas State University, was used to control what?
Grasshoppers

A getaway to a driving adventure

Beginning with its name, Wabaunsee County has always been special

Here's a Kansas trivia question for you.

What is the only county in Kansas named for an Indian chief? If you guessed Wabaunsee then you guessed right, but I bet you don't know what it means. If your answer is "dawn of day," then give yourself a big pat on the back and move to the front of your Kansas history class.

Here's the scoop according to an account in historian John Rydjord's "Indian Place-Names":

It seems that a young Potawatomi warrior sought revenge for the death of his friend who was killed by the Osage. To avenge his friend's death he crept into the enemy camp in the pre-dawn darkness and quickly dispatched a dozen Osage warriors. The account says that after completing his grisly task he ran from the camp and was heard to yell "Wah-bon-seh" — "day a little!" as he ran toward the rising sun. Legend has it that from that day forward the young warrior took the name Wabaunsee and in years to come would rise to prominence as chief of the Potawatomi tribe.

An interesting story, you say, but why should I go to Wabaunsee County? Well, pull up a chair, turn off the television and I'll tell you.

Interesting history is only the frosting on this day-trip cake. What you'll find in Wabaunsee County are loads of

Perhaps the most historic church in Kansas, the Beecher Bible and Rifle Church in Wabaunsee figured prominently in the pre-Civil War anti-slavery conflict which earned Kansas the nickname "Bloody Kansas."

beautiful and hilly back-road drives, some attractive limestone buildings and plenty of friendly folks to help guide you along the way.

Getting there is easy. If you're driving from Wichita, you should start early, pack a lunch and bring plenty of color film to record your day. The most enjoyable way to get there is to take the turnpike from Wichita to Cassoday, then drive north on K-177 to the Wabaunsee County line just north of Council Grove. A short distance after the county line, take the Alta Vista turnoff (east) into this well-kept Flint Hills town.

Alta Vista ("high view") — originally named Albion, then changed to Pike in honor of explorer Zebulon Pike — is

The interior of the Beecher Bible and Rifle Church remains much the same as it was in the 1860s.

700 miles of new adventures

Publicity-poor western Kansas has lots to offer motorists

A letter to the editor in one of our Sunday newspapers made a good point. Western Kansas has a lot to offer, but it doesn't do much to advertise its attractions.

As luck would have it, this day trip is to west and northwest Kansas, where we'll visit Scott, Logan and Gove counties. Now some of you may not want to drive 700 miles in one day, as I did. You might want to take the sane approach by driving out the afternoon before and staying the night in Scott City or Oakley. Then you can start your day trip bright and early the next day.

From Wichita you can take K-96 all the way to Scott City. Or, you can take I-135 north to McPherson, get on U.S. 56 west to Great Bend, then hook up with K-96 to Scott City.

To the south of K-96 between Ness City and Dighton is Beeler. George Washington Carver homesteaded and built a sod house near there when he was in his early 20s. He lived there for two years, then sold his claim so he could attend college. Carver had been accepted for admission at Highland College in Doniphan County, but when he arrived for classes the college refused him entrance.

Ten miles after entering Scott County you'll be at Scott City. A short distance south on U.S. 83 is White Woman Creek, which empties into White Woman Basin. All of this white woman business comes from one of several stories of how the creek came to be named.

One version has it that a despondent young woman drowned herself in the creek after the death of her sweetheart, who drowned trying to cross the creek to visit her. Another account says that a white woman, forced to become the wife of an Indian chief, killed herself after she was blamed for the death of the chief's infant son. A third says that the wife of a young Army officer was kidnapped and escaped from the Indians. Trouble was, she was never seen again. But her ghost is said to wander the banks on moonlit nights.

Fossil hunting is a popular pastime for visitors to western Kansas.

Scott City, population 4,000, is the county seat and is dead-center in the county. The site was chosen by town founder Maria DeGeer who moved there from Chicago with her daughter in 1885. According to Marilyn Walcher, Scott City librarian, DeGeer's intention was to "found a town of high moral values." She chose the location because it was the highest point around. DeGeer also founded the Western Times, the county's first newspaper.

Then things turned sour. Time came to elect city officials and DeGeer wasn't elected to anything. Irate over being unappreciated, she and her daughter packed up their belongings and moved to Sharon Springs in Wallace County.

Ten miles north on U.S. 83 is Lake Scott State Park. Aside from the fact that it's a beautiful park in a unique location, you should know that it was the first state park in Kansas. Tucked into Ladder Creek Canyon, the park has several large springs that flow together and form the 1,120-acre state fishing lake at the north end of the canyon.

Immediately past the park entrance is Big Springs, the largest of the free-flowing springs. The 56-degree water cascades from the bottom of a bluff into a small, dammed pond at the rate of 400 gallons per minute. On an experimental basis the Kansas

Department of Wildlife and Parks has stocked the pond with rainbow trout. Trout fishing is not allowed in the pond; however, trout are stocked for anglers to catch in the main lake during the trout season from mid-October through mid-April. Anglers are required to have a state trout stamp during the trout season.

Toward the center of the park is El Cuartelejo, the ruins of the only known Indian pueblo in Kansas. The Picurie Indians (from a small village near Taos) moved there in the 1600s to escape Spanish domination. They chose this valley because of its steady flow of spring water and because the surrounding bluffs offered them some protection from the elements. The Indians dug irrigation channels for their small gardens. When white settlers arrived in the 1800s they used the same channels for their crops.

Several hiking trails lead visitors from the canyon floor though sandsage prairie to the canyon rim. Panoramic views of the surrounding area make the climb worthwhile.

If you like competitive running events then show up at the park each August for the 10K and 2K races. There's also an Easter pageant held in the park in the spring.

Fall and spring weekdays are particularly good times to visit Lake Scott. Virtually every camp site is available —

you'll have the lake and trails to yourself. If you have any questions about event dates or park fees, call Park Manager Rick Stevens at (316) 872-2061.

From Lake Scott take U.S. 83 north for about 10 miles to Gove County and one of the two Chalk Pyramids turnoffs. The second turnoff is across the road from Pyramid View School, a fine old building that once served students from the surrounding area. Imagine for a moment what it must have been like to attend school there before they had paved roads or propane to heat with during the frigid winter months.

Drive east for six miles and you'll be at Monument Rocks National Landmark, also known as the Chalk Pyramids. Call them what you want, they have the distinction of being the first Kansas geological formation to be designated a National Natural Landmark by the Department of Interior.

Rising to 70 feet above the valley of the Smoky Hill River, these monoliths are a must-see attraction in western Kansas. This place is an artist's delight, so bring a camera, sketch pad or easel and have a ball recording these wonderful chalk formations. The pyramids are located on private land adjacent to a public road so don't leave any trash.

Drive back to U.S. 83 and then go north to Russell Springs in Logan County. The road there takes you across the high plains where there's a distinct possibility you will see an antelope or two if you look closely at the ridges and valleys.

Russell Springs was a way station on the Butterfield Overland Stage route. Today you can see artifacts from the stagecoach era at the Butterfield Trail Museum in the picturesque old school building. There are no gas stations in town, so be sure to fill up before heading to Russell Springs.

About a mile north of town on K-25 is one of western Kansas' stranger attractions. It doesn't cost you a dime and you don't have to stop for a visit. Keep your eyes to the west side of the road and you'll see a cowboy boot, stuck heel to the sky, on every fence post for a half-mile or so.

John Smith, a rancher north of Russell Springs, started putting boots on his fence posts because he thought it would be unique. Smith likes all things Western and this seemed to him to be the right combination of man and nature.

It wasn't long before folks from around the area got into the spirit and gave Smith their worn-out boots. Some years back television's Charles Kuralt chose Smith and his boot-covered fence posts for one of his "On the Road" segments.

A lone cottonwood glows in the late afternoon light in October, surrounded by the Chalk Beds 15 miles south of Collyer.

An RV camper is the lone occupant of a point at Lake Scott State Park. The placid 98-acre state fishing lake is a popular fishing hole for water-starved residents of western Kansas. The state park and lake are located north of Scott City.

A visitor to Lake Scott State Park takes a sunrise picture of the lake and Ladder Creek Canyon, the area surrounding the park and lake.

A visitor pauses for a moment between a large boulder and a stone shelter on the western ridge of Ladder Creek Canyon overlooking Lake Scott State Park.

Right here in River City

Wichita offers visitors a rich variety of experiences

At a glance this prairie metropolis of 310,238 folks may not strike you as a great place for a day trip. But think again. Where else in Kansas offers such a variety of experiences within such a small area?

A walk on the wild side doesn't just consist of the nighttime scene in Old Town. It also includes a number of excellent nature areas right here in River City.

One of the most established nature trails in Wichita is Pawnee Prairie Park, a wonderful bit of wilderness on the west edge of town just off U.S. 54. The park has more than six miles of outstanding nature trails along and around Cowskin Creek. The trails take an hour or two to walk and are full of natural surprises.

On Wichita's north end is Chisholm Creek Park. It has a 1 3/4 mile, handi-capped-accessible, paved nature trail. Both natural areas have water and rest room facilities. Chisholm Creek park is home to the annual "Walk With Wildlife". Each June the "Walk" draws thousands of Kansans who walk the trails to learn about natural Kansas from hundred of volunteers who establish stations along the trail. Each station deals with a particular subject; snakes, mammals, reptiles, amphibians, birds...well, you get the picture.

Bob Gress, director of the Great Plains Nature Center located at the northeast corner of Chisholm Creek Park, and his staff offer group tours of

Fireworks light the downtown sky as Wichita celebrates Riverfest.

*The bike trail along the Arkansas River through
Wichita is one of the most used attractions in the
downtown area of Wichita.*

both areas. Because of their popularity, the tours should be arranged three or four weeks in advance. Tour groups can range in size from 10 to 25. Gress says groups will learn not only about the variety of plants and animals in these areas, but also about the interrelationship of wildlife and habitat.

"Our outings are geared toward fun and education," Gress said. The tours are free, but donations to the Great Plains Nature Center are cheerfully accepted.

The GPNC is a combined project of the Wichita Parks Department, the Kansas Department of Wildlife and Parks and the U.S. Fish and Wildlife Service. The Center has a 200-seat auditorium, classrooms for seminars and presentations and a full-time staff to answer any question you might have about natural Kansas.

For those who prefer their flora a little more on the gentle side, there is Botanica, the Wichita Gardens. Botanica has grown into Kansas' botanical showplace, rich in new ideas, traditions and variety. Botanica's 9 1/2 acres include a rose garden with more than three dozen varieties, the Terrace Garden, the Margie Button Memorial Fountain surrounded by colorful annuals, a new butterfly garden and enclosure, and the Shakespeare Garden.

You can also enjoy the two-acre Woodland Walk and the more than three dozen varieties found in Botanica's juniper collection. "You would hardly know you were two blocks from downtown Wichita," said Don Buma, former director of Botanica. It's a wonderful place to walk around and explore or just sit a spell.

Then there's the Sedgwick County Zoo, one of the finest zoos in the United States. This "master plan zoo", meaning one completely planned before its construction, features the Apes and Man exhibit (ape expert Jane Goodall says she loves this place), the Pampas/Outback and its outdoor aviary with hundreds of exotic birds screeching and flitting about. The zoo also has the African Veldt (monkeys and all), the Jungle Building (an absolute must during the harsh winter months), the Herpetarium (land snakes alive!), the Asian Farm, and the American Farm with the ever-popular Children's Farm (young ones can pet the goats).

Perhaps the most popular area at the zoo is the North American Prairie Exhibit, an elevated walkway that allows you to observe an ample cross-section of prairie wildlife from above.

If that isn't enough to wear you down, you can walk yourself silly on the adjacent three-mile nature trail. Call ahead and arrange for a guided tour or pick up a pamphlet and head out on your own. The zoo also has a restaurant and gift shop. It's open seven days a week from 10 a.m. to 6 p.m.

If you've had enough of nature and are looking for your education and entertainment in air-conditioned comfort, visit the Omnisphere and Science Center in downtown Wichita. The Hands-on Science Center has two exhibit halls and is a real learning opportunity for everyone in the family. Electrifying is the key word for your visit to Challenger Hall.

Any volunteer who puts his or her hands on the Van de Graaff generator will find it a hair-raising experience as 100,000 volts of static electric discharge surges through their body. It's harmless, fun and funny.

The two halls offer more than 70 exhibits. Fifty are for children; 20 more in Challenger Hall demonstrate the principles of physics and are geared more for eighth-graders and older.

Had enough? Naaah!

History, in a very attractive package, is right next door to the Omnisphere. The Wichita Sedgwick County Historical Museum is not only one of the most impressive buildings in downtown Wichita, it's also the place where history lives on. Inside the renovated original Wichita City Hall building are displayed the history and memorabilia of Wichita and Sedgwick County.

Upriver a short distance, at the confluence of the Arkansas and Little Arkansas rivers, is the Mid-America All-Indian Center. Inside the center is a museum that offers a look at the cultures of the Plains Indians. Behind the center is the Keeper of the Plains, a magnificent metal statue of an Indian chief, arms uplifted toward the eastern sky. The impressive symbol of Wichita's original founders was designed by the late Blackbear Bosin, the well-known Native American artist from Wichita.

Directly to the west is the Wichita Art Museum, home of one of the finest collections of works by American artists. The museum and its high-quality exhibitions are must-sees on any tour of Wichita.

To wrap up your day you really ought to visit Old Cowtown Museum, just a few blocks west of the art museum. Yes, I know it's late and you should be getting home, but this place is worth the extra time. Everything you would ever want to know about Wichita from 1865 to 1880 is there for your enjoyment and education.

Tucked along the banks of the Arkansas River, this 17-acre re-creation of Wichita is alive and lively. Folks dressed in period costumes stroll the dusty streets and boardwalks to add flavor and answer questions. And there's even a brand new (original) DeVore Family Farm from the 1880s at the western edge of the complex. Call ahead to find out what's going on.

These are but a few of the things you can do and places you can go during a day trip to Kansas' largest city. All are operated by Wichita or Sedgwick County and are free or charge a nominal fee.

Botanica, the Wichita Gardens – (316) 264-0448

Mid-America All-Indian Center – (316) 262-5221

Old Cowtown Museum – (316) 264-0671

Omnisphere and Science Center – (316) 264-3174

Sedgwick County Zoo – (316) 942-2212

Wichita Art Museum – (316) 268-4921

Wichita-Sedgwick County Historical Museum – (316) 265-9314

Great Plains Nature Center – (316) 683-5499

Greensburg's hole in one

World's Largest Hand-Dug Well attracts more than 50,000 visitors each year

If Horace Greeley had known how difficult it would be to find water in the "Great American Desert," he might not have been so gung ho with his proclamation to "Go west, young man." But then again maybe he would have said it anyway. Folks were tougher back then, and pioneers were no strangers to hard times.

Families who traveled through western Kansas probably thought long and hard about watering holes before they left the moisture-laden East in pursuit of whatever dreams folks yearned to pursue in the early to mid-1800s.

Some interesting things happened when people moved into semiarid western Kansas, and one of those things turned out to be U.S. 54's biggest attraction: the World's Largest Hand-Dug Well, Greensburg's entry into the Guinness Book of World Records.

You probably know how to get there, but in case you don't you take U.S. 54 west from Wichita to Greensburg. Now, wasn't that easy?

The Big Well is one of those places that just about everyone has heard of and probably passed within two blocks of on U.S. 54, or might have actually stopped there but only looked down into the abyss through the wire mesh. But as I tell people on my bus tours, you can't say that you've really been to the well until you've walked down the 120 steps to the bottom. And that's a fact.

"Mercy sakes!" exclaimed an amazed California man as he began his descent on the steep metal stairway. Taken by the sights, he paused every 10 feet to snap pictures with his new automatic camera. "This is really something. It really takes on a different look when you get to the bottom."

And that it does.

Peering through the wire mesh at the top gives you no feel for the scope of this hand-dug excavation, a cylindrical hole some 32 feet wide by 109 feet deep. Built when Greensburg was granted a franchise for a waterworks system in 1887, the well cost $45,000, big bucks for those days.

Excavation by hand began in 1887. The work was finished in 1888 and was considered an engineering coup for that era. The native stone wall casing, quarried from the Medicine River 12 miles to the south, was constructed as dirt was removed and a circular wooden platform lowered.

The well served as Greensburg's primary water supply until 1932 and could still be called into service if it were needed. It opened as a tourist attraction in 1937. Since the well opened more than 3 million visitors have peered or walked into the "World's Largest Hand-Dug Well."

"We're an interesting place, especially when you think about that dirt being moved out of there one shovel at a time," said former gift shop manager Pennie Keller.

Even though the local folks take the big hole in the ground for granted, they are pleased with tourism that it brings to the Greensburg area.

"I was as bad as everybody else," Keller said. "I raised three kids within a block of this place, and all I did was threaten them with their lives if they went up around the well, and never bothered to come myself. I came to Greensburg in 1947 and didn't visit the well until June of 1958."

The gift shop has another famous attraction of some astronomical note as well as considerable heft. While the well is a marvel of manmade inner space, the 1,000-pound pallasite meteorite, on display in a small room off the gift shop, is a celestial marvel from outer space.

Slamming into the earth at about the time of Christ, the meteor rested undisturbed until unearthed in the 1940s on the Ellis Peck farm, six miles east of Greensburg. It is the largest pallasite meteorite ever found said Dea Anne Corns, the current gift shop manager. A smaller 700-pound meteorite, also taken from the Peck farm, is on display at the Smithsonian Museum.

According to Corns, pallasite mete-

One of the treats following a visit to Greensburg's Big Well is a trip to Clark State Fishing Lake, west of Greensburg on U.S. 54 and 10 miles south of Kingsdown.

orites are the rarest on earth, constituting only two percent of all meteorite strikes worldwide. Corns said the meteorite has drawn more people in recent years, possibly because of an increased interest in all things astronomical, as well as the recent passage of the Hale-Bopp Comet.

In 1997 Neil Armstrong, the first man to walk on the moon, visited the Big Well. However, Corns said Armstrong wasn't so much interested in the well as he was in the pallasite meteorite. Corns added that Armstrong's visit would have gone unnoticed had someone at a local convenience store not recognized him, and struck up a conversation. Corns heard about the encounter, checked the visitor's register, and sure enough, America's most famous astronaut had signed the book.

The Big Well and gift shop are open 8 a.m. to 8 p.m. daily from Memorial Day through Labor Day. The rest of the year hours are 9 a.m. to 5 p.m. Admission to the well is $1, or you can look from the top for free. If you make the trek down to the well you get a wooden token saying that you survived the journey. For more information, call Corns at (316) 723-2261.

Greensburg, the western terminus of the old "Cannonball Highway," is a great place to roam around. After visiting the well you should drop by the Hunter Drug store for an old-fashioned malt or soda drink in a drug store right out of the 1950s.

Our next stop is Clark State Fishing Lake, one of the true wonders of southwestern Kansas. As a footnote, the Cannonball Highway, from Wichita to Greensburg, was, in 1880, reputed to be the "fastest, most efficient" stagecoach line in Kansas.

From Greensburg continue west on U.S. 54 until you get to Kingsdown, supposedly named by the two Englishmen who founded the town. One of the Englishmen is said to have been looking across the soft prairie grasses, dancing on a Kansas wind, and said "It reminds me of the King's down."

From Kingsdown travel 8 1/2 miles south on K-94 and then one mile west. Be prepared for a big surprise because the canyon that cradles Clark State Fishing Lake sneaks up on you in a very pleasant way.

This isn't just another southwest Kansas fishing lake. It's very special, a prairie diamond in the rough. And you would never guess, while driving down K-94 past semiarid farmland, that the end of the road would hold 337 acres of liquid relief.

Clark State Fishing Lake, managed by the Kansas Department of Wildlife and Parks as a state fishing lake, is a glistening gem across the bottom of an area formerly known as Fatty Evans Canyon.

According to popular history, Evans was a moonshiner who ran his stills in the canyon.

Constructed by the Civilian Conservation Corps during the Depression, the lake's dam was finished in 1939. The park officially opened as a state fishing lake in 1943. The excellent fishing lake is fed at the north end by Bluff Creek. It's important to remember that the lake is for fishing only. Swimming, pleasure boating and wind surfing are not allowed.

The area surrounding the lake has six primitive camping and picnicking areas as well as fresh water for campers. The trash policy is the same as at most state fishing lakes — you pack it in, you pack it out.

A total of 1,240 acres is available to fish, hike and explore, including the J.R. Wood Memorial Nature at the north end of the lake. And there's a nice wooded area below the dam for picnicking.

If you haven't had enough pleasant surprises, then travel back to K-94 and turn south on the dirt road to Ashland. It's a good road, so don't worry about getting stuck or damaging your vehicle. This drive is one of the most scenic prairie rides you'll ever take, complete with sweeping vistas sans power lines, oil pumpers or fences.

It's open-range country, so keep in mind that cattle have the right of way. Take your time and enjoy the ride.

About three miles north of Ashland you'll notice a memorial with three crosses at the crest of a hill to the east. The marker indicates the spot where, in 1876, three Benedictine brothers came to the area from Atchison to start a monastery. The buildings were largely constructed into the sides of hills; however, the project was abandoned when the brothers were recalled to Atchison.

The memorial was built by the Clark County Council of Clubs and the date of when the monastery was active is inscribed in one of the original stones used to build the monastery. The remaining material used in the construction can be found on area farms and ranches.

At Ashland, named for Henry Clay's home in Kentucky, you can have lunch and visit the Pioneer Museum on U.S. 160 before heading west to U.S. 283, then north to St. Jacob's Well and the Big Basin.

The entry point to the basin and well is on the east side of U.S. 283 about four miles north of the U.S. 160/283 intersection.

The basin is primarily the result of underground water eating at the subsoil structure. It eventually caused the area to drop, forming a large "sink" or basin. The basin is most photogenic early or late in the day, but the real attraction is a mile or two down the road east at St. Jacob's Well.

The well is a natural sink, sort of a miniature version of the basin. It's circular, about 30 feet across, and it's nestled into a rocky hillside surrounded by ancient cottonwood trees and poison ivy to the sides of the path and around the edge of the water. If those trees could talk they probably would tell some pretty interesting stories about the folks they've seen and the things that have occurred under their aging branches.

The dark, nutrient-rich water abounds with microscopic life in addition to some mighty large frogs and turtles who make their home in and around the well's edge.

A well-defined path leads you to the well for a closer look at what was probably lifesaving water to the Plains tribes, pioneers and cowboys who made this barren landscape their home in the 1800s.

The large cottonwoods surrounding the well are the only trees in the area and must have been a welcome sight to pioneers thirsting for water, shade and a wind break as they crossed the unforgiving prairie.

There isn't much to do at the well except to experience the sights, sounds and fragrances of the prairie. It makes a great spot to arrive at late in the afternoon, set up a tent or sleep in your camper, then experience the serenity of a star-speckled night followed by a breathtaking dawn. I know, I've done it.

And if you like a good echo you might give a yell. Echoes, you ask. What would an echo be doing in the wide-open spaces?

On a calm day, if you stand on the bluff overlooking the well and give a good loud hoot, the sound will bank off the well wall, then bounce twice off adjacent basin walls. Trust me, it's a genuine three-echo experience.

Walking on the wild side

Here are some fine Kansas spots to fish, hike and enjoy Mother Nature

State Owned and Leased Areas

Almena Diversion Wildlife Area — 111 acres. 2 1/2 miles southwest of Almena.

Atchison State Fishing Lake and Wildlife Area — 179 acres. 4 miles north, 2 miles west of Atchison.

Barber State Fishing Lake and Wildlife Area — 80 acres. 1/4 mile north of Medicine Lodge.

Big Hill Wildlife Area — 1,320 acres. 8 miles west, 4 miles south of Parsons.

Blue River Wildlife Area — 35 acres. 7 miles east, 1 mile south of Washington.

Bourbon State Fishing Lake and Wildlife Area — 350 acres. 4 1/2 miles east of Elsmore.

Brown State Fishing Lake and Wildlife Area — 189 acres. 8 miles east, 1/2 mile south of Hiawatha.

Butler State Fishing Lake and Wildlife Area — 351 acres. 3 miles west, 1 mile north of Latham.

Cedar Bluff Wildlife Area — 11,834 acres. 16 miles south of WaKeeney.

Chase State Fishing Lake and Wildlife Area — 452 acres. 1 1/2 miles west of Cottonwood Falls.

Cheney Wildlife Area — 7,958 acres. 7 miles east of Pretty Prairie.

Cheyenne Bottoms Wildlife Area — 13,416 acres. 5 miles north, 5 miles east of Great Bend.

Cimarron National Grasslands Fishing Pits — 8 miles north of Elkhart.

Clark State Fishing Lake and Wildlife Area — 1,040 acres. 9 miles south, 1 mile west of Kingsdown. No migratory waterfowl hunting.

Clinton Wildlife Area — 8,090 acres. 8 miles southwest of Lawrence.

Copan Wildlife Area — 2,360 acres. 1/2 mile west of Caney.

Council Grove Wildlife Area — 2,638 acres. 5 miles northwest of Council Grove.

Cowley State Fishing Lake — 13 miles east of Arkansas City.

Crawford State Fishing Lake — 9 miles north, 1 mile east of Girard.

Douglas State Fishing Lake and Wildlife Area — 713 acres. 1 1/2 miles north, 1 mile east of Baldwin.

Elk City Wildlife Area — 10,966 acres. 3 miles west of Independence.

Fall River Wildlife Area — 8,801 acres. 14 miles northeast of Severy.

Finney Sand Pits — South edge of Garden City.

A honey bee, our state insect, flies toward a sunflower, our state wildflower.

Finney State Fishing Lake and Wildlife Area — 863 acres. 8 miles north, 3 miles west of Kalvesta.

Ford State Fishing Lake — 5 miles east, 3 miles north of Dodge City.

Geary State Fishing Lake and Wildlife Area — 195 acres. 8 1/2 miles south, 1 mile west of Junction City.

Glen Elder Wildlife Area — 12,500 acres. Tracts immediately surrounding Cawker City.

Goodman State Fishing Lake — 4 miles south, 2 1/2 miles east of Ness City.

Hain State Fishing Lake and Wildlife Area — 53 acres. 5 miles west of Spearville. Migratory bird hunting only.

Hamilton State Fishing Lake and Wildlife Area — 432 acres. 3 miles west, 2 miles north of Syracuse.

Harmon Wildlife Area — 102 acres. 1 mile north, 1 mile east of Chetopa.

Hodgeman State Fishing Lake and Wildlife Area — 254 acres. 4 miles east, 2 miles south of Jetmore.

Hollister Wildlife Area — 2,432 acres. 6 miles west, 2 miles south of Fort Scott.

Hulah Wildlife Area — 844 acres. Scattered tracts east and west of Elgin.

Jamestown Wildlife Area — 2,728 acres. 3 1/2 miles north, 2 miles west of Jamestown.

Jewell State Fishing Lake and Wildlife Area — 165 acres. 6 miles south, 3 miles west of Mankato.

John Redmond Wildlife Area (Otter Creek Arm) — 1,472 acres. 4 miles west, 2 miles north of Burlington.

Kaw Wildlife Area — 4,341 acres. 1 mile southeast of Arkansas City.

Kingman State Fishing Lake and Wildlife Area — 4,043 acres. 7 miles west of Kingman.

Kiowa State Fishing Lake — Northwest edge of Greensburg.

LaCygne State Fishing Lake and Wildlife Area — 4,080 acres. 5 miles east of LaCygne.

Lane Wildlife Area — 42 acres. 3 miles east, 6 1/2 miles north of Dighton.

Leavenworth State Fishing Lake and Wildlife Area — 376 acres. 4 miles west, 1 mile north of Tonganoxie.

Lenora Wildlife Area — 150 acres. 2 miles east of Lenora.

Logan State Fishing Lake and Wildlife Area — 271 acres. 9 miles south of Winona.

Louisberg-Middle Creek State Fishing Lake — 7 miles south of Louisberg.

Lovewell Wildlife Area — 5,215 acres. 12 miles northeast of Mankato.

Lyon State Fishing Lake and Wildlife Area — 562 acres. 5 miles west, 1 mile north of Reading.

McPherson State Fishing Lake — 6 miles north, 2 1/2 miles west of Canton.

Marais Des Cygnes Wildlife Area — 6,376 acres. 5 miles north of Pleasanton.

Marion Wildlife Area — 3,062 acres. 2 miles south, 2 miles east of Durham.

Meade State Fishing Lake and Wildlife Area — 400 acres. 8 miles south, 5 miles west of Meade.

Melvern Wildlife Area — 9,477 acres. Vicinity of Olivet and west to near Arvonia.

Miami State Fishing Lake and Wildlife Area — 267 acres. 8 miles east, 5 miles south of Osawatomie.

Milford Wildlife Area — 15,714 acres. Tract from the southwest side of Milford Dam extending up the lake to 8 miles north of Wakefield.

Mined Land Wildlife Area — 14,015 acres. Scattered tracts throughout Crawford and Cherokee counties.

Montgomery State Fishing Lake — 3 miles south, 1 mile east of Independence.

Morton Wildlife Area — 533 acres. 7 miles north of Elkhart. (Within Cimarron National Grasslands).

Nebo State Fishing Lake and Wildlife Area — 6 acres. 7 miles east, 1 mile south of Holton.

Nemaha State Fishing Lake and Wildlife Area — 710 acres. 1 mile east, 4 miles south of Seneca.

Neosho State Fishing Lake — 6 miles south, 1 mile west of St. Paul.

Neosho Wildlife Area — 2,016 acres. 1 mile east of St. Paul.

Norton Wildlife Area — 5,656 acres. 5 miles west, 2 miles south of Norton.

Osage State Fishing Lake — 3 miles south, 1/2 mile east of Carbondale.

Ottawa State Fishing Lake and Wildlife Area — 611 acres. 5 miles north, 1 mile east of Bennington.

Pottawatomie No. 1 State Fishing Lake and Wildlife Area — 190 acres. 4 1/2 miles north of Westmoreland.

Pottawatomie No. 2 State Fishing Lake and Wildlife Area — 1 1/2 miles east, 2 1/2 miles north of Manhattan.

Perry Wildlife Area — 9,534 acres. 1/2 mile west, 1 mile north of Valley Falls.

Pratt Sandhills Wildlife Area — 4,757 acres. 6 miles west, 5 miles north of Cullison.

Rooks State Fishing Lake and Wildlife Area — 243 acres. 1 1/2 miles south, 2 miles west of Stockton.

Saline State Fishing Lake — 2 1/2 miles north, 2 miles west of Salina.

St. Francis Sand Pits — 1 mile west, 2 miles south of St. Francis.

Scott Wildlife Area — 160 acres. 12 miles north of Scott City.

Sheridan State Fishing Lake — 11 miles east of Hoxie.

Sheridan Wildlife Area — 458 acres. 2 miles east, 4 miles north of Quinter.

Sherman State Fishing Lake and Wildlife Area — 1,295 acres. 10 miles south, 2 miles west of Goodland. No waterfowl hunting.

Shawnee State Fishing Lake — 7 miles north, 2 1/2 miles east of Silver Lake.

St. Francis Wildlife Area — 480 acres. 2 miles south, 2 1/2 miles west of St. Francis.

Texas Lake Wildlife Area — 560 acres. 4 miles west, 1 mile north of Cullison.

Theodore Granville Barcus Wildlife Area — 48 acres. 1 1/2 miles east, 1 mile north of Wolcott.

Toronto Wildlife Area — 4,366 acres. 1 mile south of Toronto.

Tuttle Creek Wildlife Area — 10,469 acres. Extends upriver from Randolph to 2 miles southeast of Blue Rapids.

Washington State Fishing Lake and Wildlife Area — 457 acres. 7 miles north, 3 miles west of Washington.

Webster Wildlife Area — 7,539 acres. 8 miles west of Stockton.

Wilson State Fishing Lake — 1 mile south, 1 mile east of Buffalo.

Wilson Wildlife Area — 8,039 acres. 7 miles northwest of Bunker Hill.

Woodson State Fishing Lake and Wildlife Area — 2,400 acres. 5 miles east of Toronto.

Two youngsters pause to talk as the sun sets behind them at Kanopolis Reservoir.

A Kansas classic — a setting sun next to a windmill.

Feeling up to a little exercise?

Here is almost everything you need to know about trails in Kansas. More trails are being developed every year so check with area Chambers of Commerce, city Parks and Recreation offices and Wildlife and Parks Regional offices for information on new trails.

STATE VISITOR INFORMATION CENTERS

Bonner Springs	(785) 299-2253
	I-70 westbound
Olathe	(913) 768-6155
	I-35 southbound
Topeka	(785) 296-3966
	State Capitol
Goodland	(785) 899-6695
	I-70 eastbound
Belle Plaine	(316) 488-3618
	Kansas Turnpike southbound

OTHER KANSAS VISITOR CENTERS

Fort Scott	(316) 223-3566 — U.S. 69
Concordia	(785) 243-2043 — U.S. 81
Liberal	(316) 624-1106 — U.S. 54

CORPS OF ENGINEERS, KANSAS CITY DISTRICT

Clinton Reservoir	(785) 843-7665
Hillsdale Reservoir	(785) 783-4366
Kanopolis Reservoir	(785) 546-2294
Melvern Reservoir	(785) 549-3318
Milford Reservoir	(785) 238-5714
Pomona Reservoir	(785) 453-2202
Perry Reservoir	(785) 597-5144
Tuttle Creek Reservoir	(785) 539-8511
Wilson Reservoir	(785) 658-2551

CORPS OF ENGINEERS, TULSA DISTRICT

Council Grove Reservoir	(316) 767-5195 or 5196
El Dorado Reservoir	(316) 321-9974
Elk City Reservoir	(316) 331-0315
Fall River Reservoir	(316) 658-4445
John Redmond Reservoir	(316) 364-8614
Marion Reservoir	(316) 382-2101 or 2102
Toronto Reservoir	(316) 658-4445
Big Hill Reservoir	(316) 336-2741

WILDLIFE AND PARKS REGIONAL OFFICES

Region 1 — Hays	(785) 628-8614
Region 2 — Topeka	(785) 273-6740
Region 3 — Dodge City	(316) 227-8609
Region 4 — Wichita	(316) 683-8069
Region 5 — Chanute	(316) 431-0380

OTHER HANDY PHONE NUMBERS

Chaplin Nature Center	(316) 442-7227
Cimarron National Grasslands	(316) 697-4621
Clark State Lake	(316) 369-2426
Dillon Nature Center	(316) 663-7411
Hunter Safety Trail	(785) 238-8727
Johnson County Parks and Recreation	(785) 831-3355

Konza Prairie Trail	(785) 532-6621
Lawrence Parks and Recreation	(785) 841-7722
Salina Parks Department	(785) 827-0221
Topeka Parks and Recreation	(785) 295-3838
Wichita Area Parks	(316) 264-8323
Great Plains Nature Center	(316) 683-5499
Kansas Department of Wildlife and Parks at Pratt	(316) 672-5911

HIKING TRAILS 5 MILES AND OVER

Clinton Lake — Douglas County
Northshore Hiking Trail: 8-mile hiking trail. One way.
Rockhaven Trail: 35-mile hiking and horse trails.

Garnett — Anderson County
Prairie Spirit Rail Trail: 52 miles from Ottawa to Iola.

Lawrence — Douglas County
Clinton Parkway: 8-mile bicycle, hiking and jogging trail.
Riverfront Park Trail: 10-mile bicycle, hiking and jogging trail along the Kansas River.

Perry Lake — Jefferson County
Perry Lake Hiking Trail: 30-mile loop hiking trail.

Overland Park — Johnson County
Indian Creek Parkway: 8 3/4-mile bicycle, hiking and jogging trail.

Fort Leavenworth — Leavenworth County
Blue Hiking Trail: 8-mile loop hiking trail.
Orange Hiking Trail: 19-mile loop hiking trail.
Yellow Hiking Trail: 14-mile loop hiking trail.

Elk City Lake — Montgomery County
Elk River Trail: 15-mile hiking and backpacking trail. One way. Water at the east trailhead.

Big Hill Lake — Montgomery County
Big Hill Lake Horse Trail: 20-mile horseback riding trail. May also be hiked. No water.

Pomona Lake — Osage County
Blackhawk Trail: 8-mile hiking and horseback riding trail in 110-mile park.

Tuttle Creek Lake — Riley County
Tuttle Cove Recreation Area: 5-mile nature trail.

Webster Lake — Rooks County
Webster and South Solomon River Trail: One-way 10-mile hiking and backpacking trail in Webster State Park.

HIKING TRAILS LESS THAN 5 MILES

Big Hill Lake — Montgomery County
Ruth Nixon Memorial Trail: 1-mile hiking trail (not a loop).

Cedar Bluff Lake — Trego County
Prairie Nature Trail: Cedar Bluff State Park. 3/4-mile nature trail.
Cedar Bluff State Park Trail: 1-mile hiking and nature trail.
Threshing Machine Canyon Trail: 2-mile loop. The trailhead is just west of the Prairie Nature Trail trailhead in the state park.

Cheney Lake — Reno County
Geifer Creek Nature Trail, Cheney State Park: 1/8-mile nature trail.

Clinton Lake — Douglas County
George Latham Trail: 4 1/2-mile loop hiking trail.
Coyote's Head Area: 1-mile hiking trail.
Backwoods Nature Trail: 5/8-mile loop.

Clark State Fishing Lake — Clark County
Jay R. Wood Memorial Nature Trail: 2-mile nature trail.

Council Grove Lake — Morris County
Pioneer Nature Trail: 3/4-mile nature trail.
Tall Grass Day Trail: 2 1/2-mile hiking trail. Trailhead is near Canning Creek Cove Gateshack.

Disturbed by a passerby, a winter flock of mallard drakes rises from Turkey Creek in northern Barber County.

El Dorado Lake — Butler County
Teter Nature Trail: 3/4-mile hiking and nature trail. Trailhead is near the dam.

Elk City Lake — Montgomery County
Post Oak Nature Trail: 2/3-mile nature trail. Trail is a loop.
Table Mound Hiking Trail: 2 3/4-mile hiking trail, not a loop.
Green Thumb Trail: 1-mile nature trail. This trail is a loop near Squaw Creek Campground.
Card Creek Hiking Trail: 2 1/3-mile hiking trail. This trail is a loop near Card Creek Campground.

Kanopolis Lake — Ellsworth County
Buffalo Track Canyon Trail: Sometimes called Horse Thief Canyon. 1-mile hiking and nature trail.

Melvern Lake — Osage County
Outlet Nature Trail: 1/2-mile nature and hiking trail.
Marais des Cygnes River Nature Trail: 1 1/3-mile interpretative trail.

Milford Lake — Clay County
Kansas Landscape Arboretum, Inc.: 193 acres and three nature trails, near Wakefield.
South Timber Creek Nature Trail: 3/4-mile nature trail.

Pomona Lake — Osage County
Deer Creek Nature Trail: 1/4-mile nature trail.
Witches Broom: 3/4-mile, self-guided nature trail.

John Redmond Lake — Coffey County
John Redmond Lake Walking Trail: 2-mile hiking trail.

Toronto Lake — Woodson County
Toronto State Park Hiking Trail: Four miles one way. Trailhead at Toronto Point Campground.
Holiday Hill Hiking Trail: 1/2-mile nature and hiking trail in Holiday Hill area. Trailhead near rest rooms.

Wilson Lake — Russell County
Burr Oak Nature Trail: 1/2-mile nature trail.
Rocktown Hiking Trail: 3-mile loop. Trailhead at parking lot area on east side of Rocktown.

Arkansas City — Cowley County
Chaplin Nature Center: 3 to 4 miles of hiking trails. Bring water.

Atchison — Atchison County
Forest of Friends Trail: 1/2-mile nature trail, a series of loops.

Baldwin City — Douglas County
Black Jack Primitive Trail: 1 1/2-mile hiking trail. Not a loop.

Fort Leavenworth — Leavenworth County
Fort Leavenworth Heritage Trail: 2 1/2-mile hiking trail.

Fort Riley — Geary County
The Kaw River Nature and History Trail: 1 1/8-mile loop trail. Trailhead is at the First Territorial Building.

Hesston — Harvey County
Hesston Municipal Golf Course Trail: 1-mile hiking and exercise trail.

Hutchinson — Reno County
Sand Hills State Park: 1-mile nature trail 3 miles northeast of Hutchinson; entrance is marked on U.S. 61.
Wildflower Trail: Dillon Nature Center. 1/2-mile nature trail.
Woodard Nature Trail: Dillon Nature Center. 3/4-mile nature trail.

Kingman — Kingman County
Byron Walker Wildlife Area: 1-mile nature trail. Trailhead is on U.S. 54, 7 miles west of Kingman.

Lawrence — Douglas County
Rock Creek Park Trail: 1/2-mile nature trail.
Burcham Park Trail: 1-mile nature trail.
Kaw River Trail: 4 1/2-mile hiking trail.
Martin Park Trail: 1/2-mile nature trail.
Mary's Lake Trail: 3/4-mile hiking trail, near Haskell School in the south part of Lawrence.

Naismith Valley Park Trail: 1-mile nature trail.

Leavenworth — Leavenworth County

Pilot's Knob Trail: 1-mile nature trail.
South Park Trail: 1-mile hiking trail.
V.A. Park Trail: 3- and 2-mile hiking and nature trails.

Manhattan — Riley County

Konza Prairie Trails: 4 1/2 miles of trails on the Konza Prairie. Check with the office at (785) 532-6621 for seasonal open dates.

Newton — Harvey County

Lakeside Nature Trail: 1- and 3-mile nature trails at the Harvey County West Lake.

Olathe — Johnson County

Ernie Miller Park: 3-mile nature and hiking trail which includes 1/2-mile trail for handicapped.
Waterworks Lake: 1 /2-mile hiking, bicycle and jogging trail.

Salina — Saline County

Indian Rock Natural Area: Hiking area; horseback riding allowed. No water. No overnight camping.
Lakewood Park Natural Area: 1 1/4 miles of self-guided, interconnecting trails. Picnic area. Park Office: (785) 823-1245.

Shawnee Mission — Johnson County

Shawnee Mission Park Nature Trails: 3/4- and 1/2-mile nature trails.

Topeka — Shawnee County

Dornwood Park Nature Trail: 1/2-mile loop nature trail.
Shawnee County North Community Park Trail: 1-mile nature trail.
Wells Park Nature Trail: 1-mile nature trail.
Winter Park Trail: 2-mile nature and jogging trail.

Wichita — Sedgwick County

Chisholm Creek Park, 3238 N. Oliver: 1 1/2-mile asphalt hiking trail includes water, rest rooms and picnic area.
Pawnee Prairie Park Hiking Trail: 3-mile hiking trail along Cowskin Creek.
Lake Afton Nature Trail: 2/3-mile hiking trail. One way.
Sedgwick County Zoo Nature Trail: 1/2 mile east of 13th and Ridge Road. $1 admission.

Frisco Lakes Trail — Johnson County

Hunter Safety Trail — Milford Lake

1-mile trail designed to teach safe hunting practices. May be hiked by the general public. For more information, call (785) 238-8727.

Woodland Nature Trail — Phillips County

1-mile nature trail.

BICYCLE TRAILS

Lawrence — Douglas County

Clinton Parkway: 8-mile bicycle, jogging and hiking trail from Lawrence to the dam at Clinton Lake.
Northshore Hiking and Biking Trail: 8-mile bicycle and hiking trail in Clinton State Park.
Constant Park Trail: 1/8-mile bicycle trail.
Lawrence Bicycle Route: 10-mile bicycle trail in the city.
River Front Park Trail: 10-mile bicycle, jogging and hiking trail along the Kaw River.
South Park Trail: 1/8-mile bicycle trail.

Overland Park — Johnson County

Blackbob Park Trail: 1-mile bicycle and jogging trail.
North Walnut Street Park Trail: 1-mile bicycle, hiking and jogging trail.
Waterworks Lake: 1/2-mile bicycle, hiking and jogging trail.

Topeka — Shawnee County

City of Topeka routes: 40 miles of bicycle routes through the city.

Wichita — Sedgwick County

Arkansas River Bike Route: 9-mile bicycle trail along the river in the center of Wichita.

Wichita Bike Trail: 5 1/2-mile bicycle trail along the Canal Route. Map available at any Wichita bicycle shop or from the Oz Bicycle Club.

FITNESS AND JOGGING TRAILS

El Dorado — Butler County

North Main Park Trail: 1-mile fitness trail.

Fall River Lake — Greenwood County

Fitness trail is on the west side of the lake.

Fort Scott — Bourbon County

Fort Scott Community College Jogging Trail.

Hesston — Harvey County

Hesston Municipal Golf Course: 1-mile hiking and exercise trail.

Hutchinson — Reno County

Woodard Jogging Trail: 1-mile jogging trail in Dillon Park.

Lawrence — Douglas County

Centennial Park Trail: 1-mile jogging and fitness trail.

Clinton Parkway Trail: 8-mile jogging, hiking and bicycle trail along Clinton Parkway from Lawrence to Clinton Lake.

Riverfront Park Trail: 10-mile jogging, hiking and bicycle trail along the Kaw River.

Leavenworth — Leavenworth County

Buffalo Bill Cody Memorial Park: 1/4-mile hiking trail.

Olathe — Johnson County

Arrowhead Park: Jogging trail.

Blackbob Park Trail: 1-mile jogging and bicycle trail.

North Walnut Street Park Trail: 1-mile jogging and bicycle trail.

Oregon Trail Park: 1-mile exercise course.

Prairie Center Park: Self-guided nature trail and miles of other short trails for joggers.

Waterworks Lake: 1/2-mile jogging, hiking and bicycle trail.

Overland Park — Johnson County

Heritage Park Jogging Trail.

Indian Creek Parkway: 8 3/4-mile jogging, hiking and bicycle trail.

Thomas S. Stoll Memorial Park Jogging Trail.

Topeka — Shawnee County

Winter Park Trail: 2-mile jogging and nature trail.

HORSEBACK RIDING TRAILS

Big Hill Lake

Big Hill Horse Trail: 20 to 30 miles of trails. No drinking water.

Clinton Lake — Douglas County

Rock Haven Horse Camp: 75 miles of trails on Fish and Game and Corps of Engineers property. Camping and drinking water available.

La Cygne State Park — Linn County

20 to 25 miles of trails in the park. The trailhead is near Louisburg.

Melvern Lake — Osage County

Two trails. Mileage has not been determined. Inquire at the park office — (785) 528-4900.

Perry Lake — Jefferson County

Perry Lake Horse Trails: Approximately 40 miles of trails. Trailhead is on the west side of the lake in the state park.

Pomona Lake — Osage County

Blackhawk Horse and Hiking Trail: 8-mile trail in 110-mile park.

Salina — Saline County

Indian Rock Natural Area: Horseback riding trails. Natural Area is in Salina along the cutoff channel of the Smoky Hill River. Access is from Iron Street south. The trails are steep. No water, open fires or overnight camping.

Lakewood Park Natural Area: No restriction on horseback riding in the park. Access is from Iron Street. Water is available at the picnic areas. No campfires or overnight camping without permit.

Shawnee Mission — Johnson County
Heritage Park: Horseback riding by permit only.
Shawnee Mission Horse Trails: 5 1/2 miles of trails.

Tuttle Creek Lake — Riley County
50 miles of trails. Inquire at the park office — (785) 539-7941.

Wichita — Sedgwick County
Lake Afton Horse Trails: 10 miles of trails.
Pawnee Prairie Park Stables: 3 1/2 miles of trails.

KANSAS STATE PARKS

Cedar Bluff
Box 76A
Ellis, KS 67637-0047
(785) 726-3212

Cheney
16000 NE 50th Street
Cheney, KS 67025-8487
(316) 542-3664

Clinton
798 N. 1415 Rd.
Lawrence, KS 66049
(785) 842-8562

Crawford
1 Lake Rd.
Farlington, KS 66734-4045
(316) 362-3671

El Dorado
618 NE Bluestem Rd.
El Dorado, KS 67042-8643
(316) 321-7180

Elk City
P.O. Box 945
Independence, KS 67301-0945
(316) 331-6295

Fall River
R.R. 1
Box 44
Toronto, KS 66777
(316) 637-2213

Glen Elder
Box 162A
Glen Elder, KS 67446
(785) 545-3345

Hillsdale
26001 W. 255th St.
Paola, KS 66071
(785) 783-4507

Kanopolis
200 Horsethief Rd.
Marquette, KS 67464
(785) 546-2565

Lovewell
R.R. 1
Box 66A
Webber, KS 66970
(785) 753-4971

Meade
Box K
Meade, KS 67865
(316) 873-2572

Eisenhower (Melvern)
29810 S. Fairlawn
Osage City, KS 66523-9046
(785) 528-4102

Milford
8811 State Park Rd.
Milford, KS 66514
(785) 238-3014

Mushroom Rock
(See Kanopolis listing)

Perry
Box 464A
Ozawkie, KS 66070-9802
(785) 246-3449

Pomona
22900 S. Highway 368
Vassar, KS 66543-9162
(785) 828-4933

Prairie Dog
Box 431
Norton, KS 67654-0431
(785) 877-2953

Sand Hills
4207 E. 56th
Hutchinson, KS 67502
(316) 542-3664

Scott
520 W. Scott Lake Dr.
Scott City, KS 67871-1075
(316) 872-2061

Toronto
R.R. 1, Box 44
Toronto, KS 66777-9715
(316) 637-2213

Tuttle Creek
5020B Tuttle Creek Blvd.
Manhattan, KS 66502-4408
(785) 539-7941

Webster
1285 11th Rd.
Stockton, KS 67669-8852
(785) 425-6775

Wilson
R.R. 1
Box 181
Sylvan Grove, KS 67481-99801
(785) 658-2465

An old oak tree frames the setting sun in Harvey County.

From A to W, the rank and file

A county-by-county look at how we came to be and where we're located

GENERAL COUNTY INFORMATION

ALLEN
Population—14,794
County Seat—Iola
Population—6,336

Established in 1855 and named after William Allen, a pro-slavery sympathizer who was a governor and senator of Ohio. He was said to have originated the saying "Fifty-four forty or fight."
Square miles—505
Population per square mile—30
License tag—AL

ANDERSON
Population—7,905
County Seat—Garnett
Population—3,252

Established in 1855 and named after Joseph Anderson, a Missourian who was elected to represent the Fort Scott district as a member of the Bogus Legislature. He was also a speaker pro tem of the Kansas Territorial House.
Square miles—584
Population per square mile—14
License tag—AN

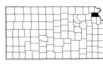

ATCHISON
Population—16,755
County seat—Atchison
Population—10,638

Established in 1855 and named after Missouri Sen. David R. Atchison, a leader in the pro-slavery movement in Kansas. He lost his Senate seat in 1855 and then led raids from Missouri against free-state settlers in Kansas. Atchison was considered to be at the forefront of efforts to make Kansas a slave state.
Square miles—431
Population per square mile—38
License tag—AT

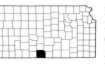

BARBER
Population—5,609
County seat—Medicine Lodge
Population—2,305

Established in 1867 and named after Thomas W. Barber, an Ohio man and free-stater who was shot to death and became a martyr after he refused to surrender when armed men stopped Barber and two friends as they rode to their homes in Lawrence. At his funeral several men, for reasons of safety, wore women's clothes so they would not be recognized by pro-slavers.
Square miles—1,136
Population per square mile—5
License tag—BA

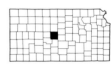

BARTON
Population—28,897
County seat—Great Bend
Population—15,144

Established in 1867 and named after nurse Clara Barton, who was called the Florence Nightingale of the Civil War. Although she had no rank or authority, she won the devotion of enlisted men and most commanders as she followed in the wake of war, healing and offering comfort to the wounded. Barton is also credited as the person who started the American Red Cross. Barton County is the only county in Kansas named after a woman.
Square miles—895
Population per square mile—32
License tag—BT

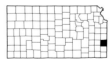

BOURBON
Population—14,863
County seat—Fort Scott
Population—8,086

Established in 1855 and named after the home county in Kentucky of Samuel A. Williams, a member of the first Kansas Legislature.

Square miles—638
Population per square mile—23
License tag—BB

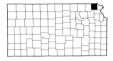

BROWN
Population—11,031
County seat—
Hiawatha
Population—3,550

Established in 1855 and named after Orville H. Browne, a prominent member of the 1855 Territorial Legislature who was described as being "brilliant and eccentric." The "e" was later dropped by the Kansas Legislature.
Square miles—572
Population per square mile—19
License tag—BR

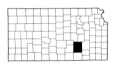

BUTLER
Population—55,736
County seat—
El Dorado
Population—12,032

Established in 1855 and named after Andrew P. Butler, a U.S. senator from South Carolina. Butler County is the largest county in Kansas and is larger than Rhode Island.
Square miles—1,443
Population per square mile—38
License tag—BU

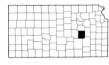

CHASE
Population—2,917
County seat—
Cottonwood Falls
Population—798

Established in 1859 and named after Ohio Gov. Salmon P. Chase, who later became chief justice of the U.S. Supreme Court. Sam Wood, a native Ohioan who became a state legislator and publisher of the first newspaper in Cottonwood Falls, was an admirer of Chase and suggested the county be named in Chase's honor. Wood was

killed in a county seat war in Stevens County.
Square miles—777
Population per square mile—4
License tag—CS

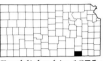

CHAUTAUQUA
Population—4,372
County seat—Sedan
Population—1,286

Established in 1875 and named after Chautauqua County, New York.
Square miles—644
Population per square mile—7
License tag—CQ

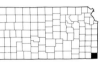

CHEROKEE
Population—22,054
County seat—
Columbus
Population—3,367

Established in 1860, it was originally named McGee after pro-slaver A.M. McGee, but was changed in 1866 to Cherokee in honor of the Cherokee Indians.
Square miles—590
Population per square mile—37
License tag—CK

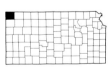

CHEYENNE
Population—3,266
County seat—
St. Francis
Population—1,442

Established in 1873 and named for the Cheyenne Indians who lived there.
Square miles—1,021
Population per square mile—3
License tag—CN

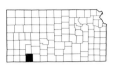

CLARK
Population—2,409
County seat—
Ashland
Population—984

Established in 1885 and named after Capt. Charles Clarke of the 6th Kansas Cavalry. The "e" was dropped by the Kansas Legislature.
Square miles—975
Population per square mile—2
License tag—CA

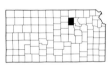

CLAY
Population—9,266
County seat—
Clay Center
Population—4,786

Established in 1857 and named after Sen. Henry Clay, a well-known Kentuckian.
Square miles—632
Population per square mile—15
License tag—CY

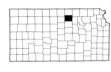

CLOUD
Population—10,516
County seat—
Concordia
Population—5,897

Established in 1867 and named after Col. William F. Cloud of the 2nd Kansas Cavalry. His Civil War battles included Wilson's Creek, Cane Hill and his defeat of the Texas "bowie knife" regiment near Van Buren, all in Arkansas. The long-haired Cloud was described by a Col. Crawford as "a nervous, vain and courageous man."
Square miles—718
Population per square mile—15
License tag—CD

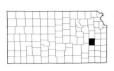

COFFEY
Population—8,651
County seat—
Burlington
Population—2,903

Established in 1855 and named after Asbury M. Coffey, member of the first Kansas Territorial Legislature who was also a colonel in the Army of the Confederacy.
Square miles—615
Population per square mile—14
License tag—CF

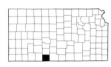

COMANCHE
Population—2,151
County seat—
Coldwater
Population—852

Established in 1867 and named for the Comanche Indians.
Square miles—789
Population per square mile—3
License tag—CM

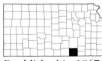

COWLEY
Population—37,240
County seat— Winfield
Population—12,090

Established in 1867 and named for Lt. Matthew Cowley of the 9th Kansas Cavalry.

A farm implement near Rock Springs 4-H Ranch glows in the early morning light.

Summertime and the livin' is easy, especially for this young angler fishing a watershed pond in Harvey County.

Cowley was killed in 1864 in a Civil War battle near Little Rock, Ark. He was said to be "loved and respected by every member of the company."
Square miles—1,128
Population per square mile—31
License tag—CL

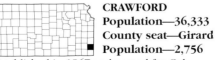

CRAWFORD
Population—36,333
County seat—Girard
Population—2,756

Established in 1867 and named for Col. Samuel J. Crawford, the third Kansas governor, who served from 1865 to 1868. Crawford par-

ticipated in the border battle of Pleasanton and had a hand in the capture of Confederate generals Marmaduke and Cabell. He also fought under the command of Gen. Nathaniel Lyon in the Battle of Wilson's Creek.
Square miles—595
Population per square mile—61
License tag—CR

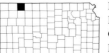

DECATUR
Population—3,586
County seat—Oberlin
Population—1,977

Established in 1873 and named for Commodore Stephen Decatur, a hero of the

Tripolitan War and the War of 1812. Decatur was described as the "most romantic and brilliant figure in the naval annals of our country." He was killed in a duel with Commodore James Barron in 1820.

Square miles—894
Population per square mile—4
License tag—DC

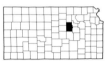

DICKINSON
Population—19,726
County seat—Abilene
Population—6,727

Established in 1857 and named after U.S. Sen. Daniel S. Dickinson of New York.

Square miles—852
Population per square mile—23
License tag—DK

DONIPHAN
Population—7,625
County seat—Troy
Population—1,049

Established in 1855 and named after Col. Alexander W. Doniphan, a pro-slaver, who organized a regiment of Missourians to fight in the Mexican War and because of his natural leadership abilities quickly rose through the ranks. Doniphan was the first county in Kansas to be named.

Square miles—388
Population per square mile—20
License tag—DP

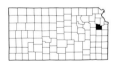

DOUGLAS
Population—88,032
County seat—
Lawrence
Population—71,721

Established in 1855 and named after Illinois Sen. Stephen A. Douglas of the famous Lincoln-Douglas debates. He authored the Kansas-Nebraska bill opening Kansas to settlement and popular sovereignty.

Square miles—461
Population per square mile—191
License tag—DG

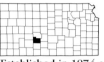

EDWARDS
Population—3,557
County seat—Kinsley
Population—1,785

Established in 1874 and named after William C. Edwards, patriarch of the Edwards family, one of the first families to settle in that area.

Square miles—620
Population per square mile—6
License tag—ED

ELK
Population—3,332
County seat—Howard
Population—852

Established in 1873 and named after the Elk River; one of the five Kansas counties named for rivers.

Square miles—650
Population per square mile—5
License tag—EK

ELLIS
Population—26,651
County seat—Hays
Population—18,632

Established in 1867 and named for 1st Lt. George Ellis, who was a member of the 12th Kansas Cavalry and fought against Quantrill's men during the Lawrence raid in 1863. He was killed in action at Jenkin's Ferry Ark., in 1864.

Square miles—900
Population per square mile—30
License tag—EL

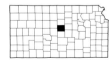

ELLSWORTH
Population—6,459
County seat—
Ellsworth
Population—2,827

Established in 1867 and named after 2nd Lt. Allen Ellsworth of the 7th Iowa Cavalry. Ellsworth was the commander at Fort Ellsworth in 1864. The fort, on the banks of the Smoky Hill River, was established before either the town or county were named.

Square miles—717
Population per square mile—9
License tag—EW

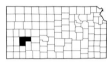

FINNEY
Population—34,726
County seat—
Garden City
Population—24,902

Established in 1873 and named after David W. Finney, a Civil War veteran who hailed from Indiana and later became lieutenant governor of Kansas. He also served several terms in the Kansas Legislature.

Square miles—1,302
Population per square mile—27
License tag—FI

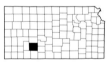

FORD
Population—28,477
County seat—
Dodge City
Population—22,033

Established in 1867 and named after Civil War veteran Capt. James H. Ford of the 2nd Colorado Cavalry. He commanded troops against the Plains Indians in the Dodge City area and was later directed by Gen. Grenville Dodge to build Fort Dodge.

Square miles—1,099
Population per square mile—26
License tag—FO

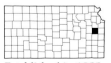

FRANKLIN
Population—23,208
County seat—Ottawa
Population—11,419

Established in 1855 and named after none

other than Benjamin Franklin, the famous inventor, politician, philosopher and all-around great guy in American history.

Square miles—577
Population per square mile—40
License tag—FR

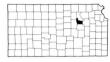

GEARY
Population—31,099
County seat—
Junction City
Population—20,380

Established in 1889 and named after John W. Geary, third territorial governor of Kansas. In 1855 it was first named Davis County after Jefferson Davis, U.S. secretary of war from 1853 to 1857, and later the chief architect of the Confederate States of America. After the Civil War, Kansas legislators changed the name at the request of Davis Countians who didn't want their county named after the president of the Confederacy.

Square miles—377
Population per square mile—83
License tag—GE

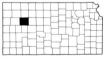

GOVE
Population—3,162
County seat—Gove
Population—99

Established in 1868 and named after Capt. Grenville L. Gove of the 11th Kansas Cavalry. Gove's Company G had the reputation of being the best-drilled company in the 11th. He died of brain fever at Olathe in 1864.

Square miles—1,072
Population per square mile—3
License tag—GO

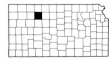

GRAHAM
Population—3,390
County seat—
Hill City
Population—1,768

Established in 1867 and named after Capt. John L. Graham of the 8th Kansas Cavalry. He was killed in action at the Battle of Chickamauga in Georgia in 1863.

Square miles—898
Population per square mile—4
License tag—GH

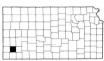

GRANT
Population—7,676
County seat—Ulysses
Population—5,859

Established in 1873 and named after Gen. Ulysses S. Grant.

Square miles—575
Population per square mile—13
License tag—GT

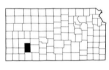

GRAY
Population—5,380
County seat—
Cimarron
Population—1,715

Established in 1887 and named after Alfred Gray, secretary of the state Board of Agriculture from 1873 to 1880.

Square miles—868
Population per square mile—6
License tag—GY

GREELEY
Population—1,803
County seat—Tribune
Population—917

Established in 1873 and named after Horace Greeley, writer for the New York Tribune and known for uttering the phrase "Go west, young man." Greeley was the last of Kansas' 105 counties to be created. Virtually every town in Greeley County had some connection with the writer—Greeley Center, Horace, Tribune and Hector, named after Greeley's dog.

Square miles—778
Population per square mile—2
License tag—GL

GREENWOOD
Population—7,995
County seat—Eureka
Population—2,884

Established in 1855 and named after Alfred B. Greenwood, U.S. land commissioner. Greenwood County is noted cattle country, with more than 75,000 head of beef cattle grazing on the county's 739,000 acres.

Square miles—1,135
Population per square mile—7
License tag—GW

HAMILTON
Population—2,311
County seat—
Syracuse
Population—1,541

Established in 1873 and named by the New Yorkers who settled there for Alexander Hamilton, one of the authors of The Federalist papers. Hamilton served on George Washington's cabinet as the first U.S. secretary of the treasury. He died in his late 40s in a famous duel with Aaron Burr.

Square miles—998
Population per square mile—2
License tag—HM

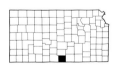

HARPER
Population—6,694
County seat—
Anthony
Population—2,376

Established in 1867 and named after 1st Sgt. Marion Harper of the 2nd Kansas Cavalry. He died from wounds sustained at Waldron, Ark., in December 1863. It was said that when he was brought in wounded he bet another man that he would be dead within so many hours.

A yellow sulfur butter-fly pauses to extract food from a musk thistle plant.

Marion Harper won his bet.
Square miles—802
Population per square mile—8
License tag—HP

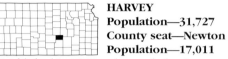

HARVEY
Population—31,727
County seat—Newton
Population—17,011

Established in 1872 and named after James M. Harvey, who served as Kansas governor from 1869 to 1873 and U.S. senator from 1874 to 1877.
Square miles—540
Population per square mile—59
License tag—HV

HASKELL
Population—3,994
County seat—Sublette
Population—1,423

Established in 1887 and named after Dudley C. Haskell, a member of the Kansas House of Representatives in 1872 and again from 1875 to 1876. He was elected U.S. representative from 1877 to 1883.
Square miles—578
Population per square mile—7
License tag—HS

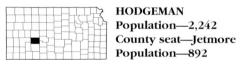

HODGEMAN
Population—2,242
County seat—Jetmore
Population—892

Established in 1873 and named after Capt. Amos Hodgeman of the 7th Kansas Cavalry. Hodgeman met and married a Leavenworth barmaid named Kitty. They were said to be very happy. She joined him at Corinth, Miss., near Shiloh. Hodgeman was killed in action in October 1863, and Kitty, under a flag of truce, was able to cross the lines and retrieve his body for burial. She later became a nurse in a Cincinnati hospital but soon weakened and died.

Sand hill plums are the basic ingredient for one of Kansas' sweetest products, homemade sand hill jelly.

Square miles—860
Population per square mile—3
License tag—HG

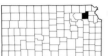

JACKSON
Population—11,634
County seat—Holton
Population—3,253

Established in 1859 and first named Calhoun in 1855 by pro-slavers who believed in the ideas of Sen. John C. Calhoun of South Carolina. The free-state legislature renamed the county in 1859 to honor President Andrew Jackson, an arch rival of Calhoun.
Square miles—658
Population per square mile—18
License tag—JA

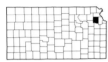

JEFFERSON
Population—16,822
County seat—
Oskaloosa
Population—1,122

Established in 1855 and named after President Thomas Jefferson. Historians in Jefferson County claim that its first settler — Daniel Morgan Boone, the son of Daniel Boone — was the first settler in Kansas in 1827. He was commissioned by the U.S. government to instruct the Indians on agricultural methods.
Square miles—535
Population per square mile—31
License tag-JF

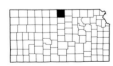

JEWELL
Population—3,943
County seat—
Mankato
Population—977

Established in 1867 and named after Lt. Col. Lewis R. Jewell of the 6th Kansas Cavalry. A member of Jewell's family founded Arcadia, in Crawford County, and it was there that Jewell returned after a stint at being a forty-niner. He was a fearless soldier who was said to have charged recklessly into Gen. John Sappington Marmaduke's Confederates. During the charge he was wounded, had a horse shot out from under him and fought on foot until he was killed by a minie ball during the battle at Cane Hill, Ark., in 1862.
Square miles—910
Population per square mile—4
License tag—JW

JOHNSON
Population—392,272
County seat—Olathe
Population—72,455

Established in 1855 and named after a Virginia slave owner, the Rev. Thomas Johnson. Johnson established the Shawnee Methodist Mission there in 1829 and was killed by an assassin at his home in 1865. Johnson Countians consistently have had the highest per capita income in Kansas.
Square miles—478
Population per square mile—821
License tag—JO

KEARNY
Population—4,139
County seat—Lakin
Population—2,156

Established in 1873 and named for Gen. Philip Kearny. Kearny's father wanted him to become a preacher, but Kearny loved the military and looked forward to the day he would lead a cavalry charge. He got his wish when he led a charge at Churubusco during the Mexican War. It cost him an arm. He took the loss well, however, and was quoted as advising his servant to "never lose your arm; it makes it hard to put on your gloves." The one-armed general was later killed during the battle of Chantilly, Va., in 1862 when he rode into a line of Confederate infantry.

Square miles—868
Population per square mile—5
License tag—KE

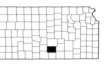

KINGMAN
Population—8,468
County seat—
Kingman
Population—3,302

Established in 1872 and named after Samuel A. Kingman, chief justice of the Kansas Supreme Court. Kingman became president of the Kansas Bar Association and the first president of the Kansas State Historical Society.
Square miles—865
Population per square mile—10
License tag—KM

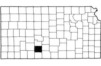

KIOWA
Population—3,605
County seat—
Greensburg
Population—1,747

Established in 1886 and named after the Kiowa Indians who had a reputation as great horsemen and who were among the last of the Plains Indians to come to Kansas.
Square miles—723
Population per square mile—5
License tag—KW

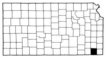

LABETTE
Population—23,149
County seat— Oswego
Population—1,927

Established in 1867 and named after Pierre La Bete. He was a Cajun hunter, trader and guide who came to Kansas in the early 1800s and settled near a creek that was later named Labette Creek. La Bete, as his name was really spelled, married an Osage woman.
Square miles—653
Population per square mile—35
License tag—LB

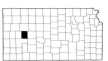

LANE
Population—2,322
County seat— Dighton
Population—1,342

Established in 1873 and named after James H. Lane, a fiery leader in the Free State Party. When Missouri ruffians blocked the gateway to Kansas, Lane brought settlers to Kansas from Nebraska and Iowa on what was known as Lane's Trail. He was described as "tall, lean, lanky, swarthy and hungry-looking," a description befitting a man with long, unruly hair who wore a bearskin coat and a calfskin vest. In the end Lane would have a county, a spring, a fort and a university at Lecompton named after him. He also served as a U.S. senator from Kansas.
Square miles—717
Population per square mile—3
License tag—LE

LEAVENWORTH
Population—68,853
County seat—
Leavenworth
Population—42,250

Established in 1855 and named after Col. Henry R. Leavenworth, who established Fort Leavenworth in 1827. One of the first counties organized in Kansas, Leavenworth County was sliced out of the Delaware Trust lands, which, by the way, belonged to the Delaware Indians. Although some of these claims could be disputed, Leavenworth County says it had the state's first fort, post office, newspaper and territorial governor's home.
Square miles—463
Population per square mile—149
License tag—LV

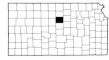

LINCOLN
Population—3,454
County seat—Lincoln
Population—1,274

Established in 1867 and named after Abraham Lincoln. The county is one of 22 (23 if you count Lincoln Parish in Louisiana) in the United States named after Lincoln.
Square miles—720
Population per square mile—5
License tag—LC

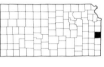

LINN
Population—8,571
County seat—
Mound City
Population—806

Established in 1867 and named after Dr. Lewis F. Linn, a U.S. senator from Missouri. One Linn County claim to fame is producing the first female rural mail carrier in the United States. Mary Hazelbaker delivered mail from 1904 until she retired in 1933.
Square miles—601
Population per square mile—14
License—LN

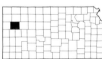

LOGAN
Population—3,145
County seat—Oakley
Population—2,106

Established in 1881 and originally named after John P. St. John, governor of Kansas. It was changed to Logan in honor of Gen. John A. Logan, a Civil War veteran from Illinois who later served in the U.S. Senate and was a vice presidential candidate. Logan and his running mate, James G. "Jingo Jim" Blaine, lost to Democrat Grover Cleveland.
Square miles—1,073
Population per square mile—3
License tag—LG

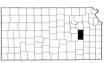

LYON
Population—34,704
County seat— Emporia
Population—25,522

Established in 1862 and named after Gen.

Nathaniel Lyon, an abolitionist who commanded the troops at Fort Riley in 1860. Later, during the Civil War, he led regiments from Kansas and Iowa in the Battle of Wilson's Creek where he was killed in action.
Square miles—844
Population per square mile—41
License tag—LY

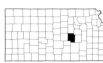

MARION
Population—13,077
County seat—Marion
Population—1,977

Established in 1855 and named after Francis Marion, an American Revolutionary War hero from South Carolina who was nicknamed the "Swamp Fox."
Square miles—944
Population per square mile—14
License tag—MN

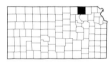

MARSHALL
Population—11,271
County seat—
Marysville
Population—3,275

Established in 1855 and named after Francis J. "Frank" Marshall. He operated a ferry and trading post at Independence Ford on the Big Blue River about nine miles below the Marysville crossing. He was said to be one of Kansas' first settlers.
Square miles—878
Population per square mile—13
License tag—MS

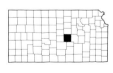

McPHERSON
Population—28,101
County seat—
McPherson
Population—12,937

Established in 1867 and named after Gen. James Birdseye McPherson, a Union general

who was killed in action at Atlanta, Ga., in 1864. McPherson was a stellar student at West Point, graduating at the head of his class. A stately statue of McPherson astride his horse stands near the beautiful county courthouse at McPherson.

Square miles—900
Population per square mile—31
License tag—MP

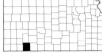

MEADE
Population—4,289
County seat—Meade
Population—1,545
Established in 1873 and named after Gen. George G. Meade, commander of the Army of the Potomac who scored big in defeating the Rebs at Gettysburg. Meade was described by those who knew him as "lacking in cordiality and disliked by his subordinates." However, he did have at least one fan in Kansas, who named a county in his honor.

Square miles—979
Population per square mile—4
License tag—ME

A thunderhead boils in from the east over a field of commercial sunflowers.

Several horses are spooked by a hot air balloon as it drifts quietly over a Sedgwick County farm.

MIAMI
Population—24,722
County seat—Paola
Population—5,527
Established in 1855 and named after the Miami Indians who lived in that area. Miami is the Indian word for mother. The county was originally named Lykins until the name was changed in 1861.
Square miles—590
Population per square mile—42
License tag—MI

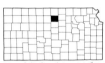

MITCHELL
Population—7,080
County seat—Beloit
Population—4,052
Established in 1867, it was named after Capt. William Mitchell who was killed shortly before the end of the Civil War at Monroe's Cross Roads, N.C. Mitchell had moved to Kansas from Massachusetts with his parents in 1855 and settled near Ogden.
Square miles—717
Population per square mile—10
License tag—MC

MONTGOMERY
Population—37,706
County seat—Independence
Population—9,909
Established in 1867 and named after either James M. Montgomery, an abolitionist who settled in Linn, or Gen. Richard Montgomery who was killed in the Battle of Quebec in 1775. Montgomery County has produced the likes of Alf Landon, Laura Ingalls Wilder, explorers Martin and Osa Johnson, playwright William Inge, oilman Harry Sinclair and movie actor Tom Mix.
Square miles—646
Population per square mile—58
License tag—MG

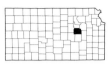

MORRIS
Population—6,321
County seat—Council Grove
Population—2,278
Established in 1859 and named after Thomas Morris, U.S. senator from Ohio. It was originally called Wise County in 1855 but the Legislature changed the name to Morris in 1859.
Square miles—693
Population per square mile—9
License tag—MR

MORTON
Population—3,399
County seat—Elkhart
Population—2,265
Established in 1886 and named for—take a deep breath—Oliver Hazard Perry Morton, the governor of and senator from Indiana. The 108,000-acre Cimarron National Grasslands in Morton County is the largest tract of public land in Kansas.
Square miles—731
Population per square mile—5
License tag—MT

NEMAHA
Population—10,443
County seat—Seneca
Population—1,991
Established in 1855 and named after the Nemaha River in Nebraska which drains the northern half of the county.
Square miles—719
Population per square mile—15
License tag—NM

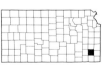

NEOSHO
Population—16,969
County seat—Erie
Population—1,278
Established in 1861 and named after the Neosho River, an Indian name meaning

"muddy waters" or "water made muddy" or, if you please, the more pleasant Osage Indian interpretation of "Water-Like-the-Skin-of-a-Summer-Cow-Wapiti." The county was originally called Dorn but the name was changed in 1861.
Square miles—576
Population per square mile—29
License tag—NO

NESS
Population—3,840
County seat—Ness City
Population—1,638
Established in 1867 and named after Cpl. Noah V. Ness of the 7th Kansas Calvary. Ness died of wounds received in battle in 1864. For a short time inventor George Washington Carver homesteaded in the vicinity of Beeler in Ness County before moving to the south and discovering the many uses of the peanut.
Square miles—1,074
Population per square mile—4
License tag—NS

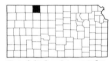

NORTON
Population—5,744
County seat—Norton
Population—2,906
Established in 1867 and named after Capt. Orloff Norton of the 15th Kansas Cavalry who was killed at Cane Hill, Ark., in 1865. N.H. Billings wanted the county named after him and got his way for a short time when the Legislature changed it in 1873. However, in 1874 the Legislature changed it back to Norton.
Square miles—873
Population per square mile—7
License tag—NT

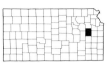

OSAGE
Population—16,325
County seat—Lyndon
Population—1,065

Established in 1859 and originally named Weller County, it was changed to Osage in 1859 for the Osage Nation. The Osage moved to Kansas when Missouri became a state in 1821. Osage County is on what was Osage land.
Square miles—695
Population per square mile—23
License tag—OS

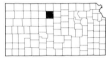

OSBORNE
Population—4,695
County seat— Osborne
Population—1,744

Established in 1867 and named after Sgt. Vincent B. Osborne of the 2nd Kansas Cavalry. Osborne survived the Civil War and settled in Ellsworth where he practiced law and helped organize Ellsworth County. Osborne County holds a unique spot in the hearts of mapmakers: It is the geodetic center of North America. The cross hairs engraved on a bronze plaque planted in the middle of a pasture is the point where one-sixth of the world's surface is measured from.
Square miles—882
Population per square mile—5
License tag—OB

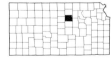

OTTAWA
Population—5,635
County seat— Minneapolis
Population—1,940

Established in 1860 and named for the Ottawa Indians, well-known intertribal traders. Ottawa signifies "to trade" or to "buy and sell." Land in Ottawa County was originally set aside for the Kansa Indians. However, they were moved south to Council Grove in 1846 and eventually ended up in Oklahoma.
Square miles—721
Population per square mile—8
License tag—OT

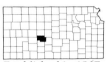

PAWNEE
Population—7,521
County seat—Larned
Population—4,474

Established in 1867 and named for the Pawnee Indians, a fierce, warlike nation that roamed freely from the Rocky Mountains to the plains of Kansas. Diseases and warring with other tribes reduced their population significantly by the late 1800s.
Square miles—755
Population per square mile—10
License tag—PN

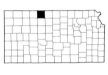

PHILLIPS
Population—6,362
County seat— Phillipsburg
Population—2,711

Established in 1867 and named after William Phillips, a lawyer from Leavenworth who was assassinated by pro-slavers who told him that all abolitionists must leave Leavenworth or they would "leave for eternity." Phillips refused, so they seized him, shaved one side of his head, stripped off his clothes, tarred and feathered him, rode him on a rail for a mile and a half and then had a black auctioneer mock Phillips by selling him for a dollar. His captors then took him to his home and killed him.
Square miles—887
Population per square mile—7
License tag—PL

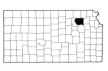

POTTAWATOMIE
Population—17,407
County seat— Westmoreland
Population—639

Established in 1857 and named for the Potawatomi tribe of Indians. Their reservation once covered much of the county. The spellings of the tribe and the county are different.
Square miles—828
Population per square mile—21
License tag—PT

PRATT
Population—9,605
County seat—Pratt
Population—6,701

Established in 1867 but officially organized in 1859, the county was named after 2nd Lt. Caleb Pratt of the 2nd Kansas Cavalry. He was one of many Kansans killed in the Battle of Wilson's Creek. Pratt was one of several counties fraudulently established in 1867 by a group of men from Hutchinson who went through the countryside setting up counties that had no bona fide residents.
Square miles—735
Population per square mile—13
License tag—PR

RAWLINS
Population—3,299
County seat—Atwood
Population—1,342

Established in 1873 and named after Gen. John A. Rawlins, a lawyer from Illinois who became a trusted adviser of Lincoln and later President Grant's secretary of war. He was described as "a teetotaler who was punctual,

Visitors to northwest Kansas rest for a while on the plateau overlooking Castle Rock in Gove County.

precise and abstemious to the verge of fanaticism."
Square miles—1,069
Population per square mile—3
License tag—RA

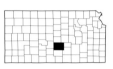

RENO
Population—62,551
County seat—
Hutchinson
Population—39,770

Established in 1867 and named after Gen. Jesse L. Reno, who was shot out of his saddle and killed during a surprise attack by Confederate soldiers at South Mountain, Md., in September 1862. Kansas has the only county in the United States that bears his name. However, Reno, Nev., was named for Gen. Reno.
Square miles—1,259
Population per square mile—50
License tag—RN

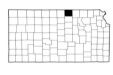

REPUBLIC
Population—6,240
County seat—
Belleville
Population—2,361

Established in 1860 and named after the Republican River because it is the first county the river flows into when it enters Kansas.
Square miles—719
Population per square mile—9
License tag—RP

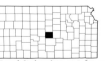

RICE
Population—10,321
County seat—Lyons
Population—3,494

Established in 1867 and named after Gen. Samuel A. Rice, a former steamboat pilot on the Ohio River who studied law and became the attorney general of Ohio. He was killed at

Two waterfowlers gather their decoys after a successful goose and duck hunt on the Arkansas River west of Wichita.

the Battle of Jenkin's Ferry in Arkansas in 1864.
Square miles—728
Population per square mile—14
License tag—RC

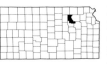

RILEY
Population—73,119
County seat—
Manhattan
Population—43,836

Established in 1855 and named after the military post Fort Riley. Because of numerous changes in the county boundary lines, Riley has possibly the most irregular shape of any county in Kansas.
Square miles—593
Population per square mile—123
License tag—RL

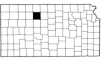

ROOKS
Population—5,936
County seat—
Stockton
Population—1,503

Established in 1867 and named in honor of Private John C. Rooks of the 11th Kansas Cavalry, who was killed during the Battle of Prairie Grove, Ark., in 1862. Rooks, who served only 100 days before being killed, is the only private to have a county in Kansas named in his honor.
Square miles—888
Population per square mile—7
License tag—RO

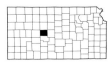

RUSH
Population—3,566
County seat—
LaCrosse
Population—1,384

Established in 1867 and named after Capt. Alexander Rush of the 2nd Kansas Colored Cavalry. Rush was killed in the Battle of

Jenkins' Ferry, Ark., in 1864. The Confederate soldiers were under orders to take no prisoners.
Square miles—718
Population per square mile—5
License tag—RH

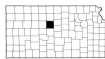

RUSSELL
Population—7,668
County seat—Russell
Population—4,760

Established in 1867 and named after Capt. Avra P. Russell of the 2nd Kansas Cavalry. Russell's family was reputed to have a long and noble bloodline that went back to Olaf, King of Rerick, in the sixth century and to some guy named Hugh who served under William the Conqueror. Russell's youngest brother, Oscar, served with the Confederacy and was near the Battle of Prairie Grove, Ark., when Avra was felled by the first Confederate volley. Oscar was permitted to cross the lines to see Avra before he died. Russell's sword is owned by the Kansas Museum of History in Topeka.
Square miles—869
Population per square mile—9
License tag—RS

SALINE
Population—51,434
County seat—Salina
Population—44,167

Established in 1860 and named after the Saline River which meanders through the county. Two Frenchmen, the Mallet brothers, originally called it the Riviere de la Fleche, or River of the Arrow. The Indians called it Ne Miskua, or Salt River, which the French translated to Saline. Because they were impressed with its size, they called it the Grande Saline.
Square miles—721
Population per square mile—71
License tag—SA

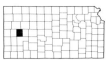

SCOTT
Population—5,157
County seat—
Scott City
Population—3,731

Established in 1873 and named after Gen. Winfield Scott, a veteran of the War of 1812, the Black Hawk War and the Seminole War. He was in command of the troops who moved the Cherokees to Indian Territory over what became known as the Trail of Tears. Scott was a Virginian whose nickname was "Old Fuss and Feathers." Fort Scott is also named in his honor.
Square miles—718
Population per square mile—8
License tag—SC

SEDGWICK
Population—419,369
County seat—Wichita
Population—310,238

Established in 1867 and named after Maj. Gen. John Sedgwick, who was originally from Cornwall Hollow, Conn. Sedgwick had a distinguished military career that included action against the Seminoles. He fought in all of the major battles in the Mexican War and was wounded at Antietam. He was said to hate hospitals and hoped that if he ever got shot again it would kill him outright. He got his wish when a Confederate sharpshooter put a minie ball in his forehead while he was inspecting his lines during the Battle of the Wilderness near Spottsylvania, Va., in 1864. Wichita, the county seat, is the largest city in Kansas.
Square miles—1,007
Population per square mile—416
License tag—SG

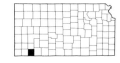

SEWARD
Population—19,123
County seat—Liberal
Population—16,949

Established in 1873 and named in honor of William Seward, Lincoln's secretary of state and an ardent supporter of statehood for Kansas. In 1861 the Legislature honored Seward's support by changing the name of Godfrey County to Seward. However, in 1867 during postwar reorganization Seward County was renamed for Gen. Oliver O. Howard. In 1873 Seward was given a second shot at eternal fame when a county between Meade and Stevens was named after him. For a short time Howard had a county named after him. It later became Chautauqua and Elk counties, and Howard had to settle for a county seat bearing his name.
Square miles—640
Population per square mile—30
License tag—SW

SHAWNEE
Population—165,122
County seat—Topeka
Population—120,645
Established in 1855 and named for the Shawnee Indians who were driven from their homes in the East by Iroquois and the white man. Thomas Johnson, who founded the Shawnee Mission, had suggested the name of Shawnee for the county he lived in, but it was named in his honor. Topeka, which means "a good place to pick potatoes," became the state capital and the county seat.
Square miles—549
Population per square mile—301
License tag—SN

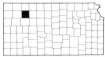

SHERIDAN
Population—2,826
County seat—Hoxie
Population—1,279
Established in 1873 and named after Gen. Philip H. Sheridan, a Civil War officer nicknamed "Little Phil" who became a military success when the Army of the Cumberland

captured Missionary Ridge during the Battle of Chattanooga. Sheridan spent several postwar years in command of troops in Kansas.
Square miles—896
Population per square mile—3
License tag—SD

SHERMAN
Population—6,886
County seat—Goodland
Population—5,034
Established in 1873 and named after Gen. William Tecumseh Sherman, a West Point graduate who will be forever remembered by Civil War historians for his famous march from "Atlanta to the sea." Sherman was known for his close association with another unheralded Kansan, Mary "Mother" Bickerdyke, a Civil War nurse from Kansas who brought medicine, food and comfort to Sherman's troops. A museum honoring Bickerdyke's efforts is at Bunker Hill in Russell County. After the war Sherman was assigned the responsibility of crushing Indian resistance in Kansas, a job he relished because he saw the Indians as enemies.
Square miles—1,057
Population per square mile—7
License tag—SH

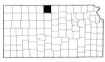

SMITH
Population—4,806
County seat—Smith Center
Population—1,956
Established in 1867 and named after Maj. J. Nelson Smith of the 2nd Colorado Cavalry. Smith was killed while leading his men in a charge on the Confederates at the Battle of the Blue near Kansas City, Mo., in October 1864. On a less honorable note, L.T. Reese, a county pioneer, is said to have organized the

county by using fraudulent names of friends back East.
Square miles—897
Population per square mile—5
License tag—SM

STAFFORD
Population—5,232
County seat—St. John
Population—1,335
Established in 1867 and named for Capt. Lewis Stafford of the 1st Kansas Infantry. Stafford was among the thousands of Union soldiers incarcerated in the infamous Andersonville prison. He was later killed at Young's Point in Louisiana.
Square miles—788
Population per square mile—7
License tag—SF

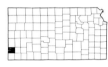

STANTON
Population—2,299
County seat—Johnson City
Population—1,326
Established in 1873 and named for Edwin M. Stanton, secretary of war under presidents Lincoln and Johnson. He was a self-centered, critical man whom Lincoln once called the "original gorilla." When President Johnson tried to have him dismissed he is said to have refused to resign and locked himself in his office.
Square miles—681
Population per square mile—3
License tag—ST

STEVENS
Population—5,177
County seat—Hugoton
Population—3,240
Established in 1873 and named after Thaddeus Stevens, a Pennsylvania congress-

*Pre-sunrise rays project
skyward over Sunrise
Lake in eastern
Harvey County.*

man who was born in Vermont, educated at Dartmouth and became a strong opponent of slavery. He was one of the architects of the impeachment of President Johnson. To back up his antislavery position he asked to be buried in a cemetery open to both blacks and whites.
Square miles—727
Population per square mile—7
License tag—SV

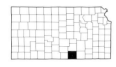

SUMNER
Population—26,436
County seat—
Wellington
Population—8,575

Established in 1867 and named after Charles Sumner, a senator from Massachusetts who was beaten up on the floor of the U.S. Senate in 1856 for his antislavery views. Sumner County is consistently the leading producer of wheat in Kansas.
Square miles—1,183
Population per square mile—22
License tag—SU

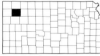

THOMAS
Population—8,341
County seat—Colby
Population—5,625

Established in 1873 and named after Brig. Gen. George H. Thomas, a West Point graduate from Virginia who fought on the Union side. He was nicknamed the "Rock of Chickamauga" for his defense of that strategic position. He commanded the 1st Kansas Battery at Nashville. The counties surrounding Thomas are also named for distinguished generals.
Square miles—1,075
Population per square mile—8
License tag—TH

Each fall thousands of Monarch butterflies stop to feed and rest in Kansas during their migration to Mexico.

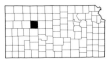

TREGO
Population—3,470
County seat—
WaKeeney
Population—2,016

Established in 1867 and named after Capt. Edward R. Trego of the 8th Kansas Infantry. During the Battle of Chickamauga Trego lost half of his men. After an evening meal he received permission to search for his wounded. During his mission he ran into a Confederate squad and was killed. His body is buried among the thousands of Union soldiers killed at Chickamauga.
Square miles—890
Population per square mile—4
License tag—TR

WABAUNSEE
Population—6,638
County seat—Alma
Population—872

Established in 1855 and named after Wabaunsee, the great Potawatomi chief. Wabaunsee is the only Kansas county to be named for an Indian.
Square miles—797
Population per square mile—8
License tag—WB

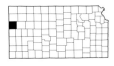

WALLACE
Population—1,816
County seat—
Sharon Springs
Population—871

Established in 1868 and named after Brig. Gen. William Harvey Lamb Wallace, who fought the Confederates at Hornet's Nest near Shiloh and was killed in action at Shiloh in April 1862.
Square miles—914
Population per square mile—2
License tag—WA

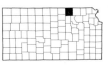

WASHINGTON
Population—6,810
County seat—
Washington
Population—1,277

Established in 1857 and named after none other than George Washington, our founding father, and the most popular choice among political place names in the United States, according to historian John Rydjord.
Square miles—898
Population per square mile—8
License tag—WS

WICHITA
Population—2,886
County seat—Leoti
Population—1,802

Established in 1873 and named by Marshall Murdock, editor of The Wichita Eagle, for the Wichita Indians. The name Wichita has generally been accepted as meaning "scattered lodges."
Square miles—719
Population per square mile—4
License tag—WH

WILSON
Population—10,314
County seat—
Fredonia
Population—2,583

Established in 1855 and named after Col. Hiero T. Wilson, the first white settler in the Fort Scott area and a successful trader. He became postmaster at Fort Scott and served as a delegate to the Lecompton Constitutional Convention. He could speak Osage, Cherokee and Creek and was known to the Osage as "Big White Chief."
Square miles—575
Population per square mile—18
License tag—WL

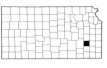

WOODSON
Population—4,020
County seat—
Yates Center
Population—1,737

Established in 1855 and named after Daniel Woodson, secretary of the territory of Kansas in 1855 and 1866. He once served as acting territorial governor.
Square miles—498
Population per square mile—8
License tag—WO

WYANDOTTE
Population—155,072
County seat—
Kansas City
Population—144,266

Established in 1859 and named for the Wyandot Indians who bought the area from the Delaware Indians. Having only 149 square miles, Wyandotte is the smallest county in Kansas. A clerical error may have caused the addition of the "te" to Wyandot.
Square miles—149
Population per square mile—1,041
License tag—WY

Did You Know?

Marshall Murdock, early publisher of The Wichita Eagle, financed a Broadway show that became a success. What was the play?
"Enter Madame"

What was the name of the car built in Wichita?
The Jones Six

Where is Buffalo Bill Mathewson buried?
Highland Cemetery, Wichita

How many covered wagons are on the Great Seal of Kansas?
Two

The Museum of Natural History in Lawrence displays an unusual exhibit from the Battle of Little Big Horn. What is it?
U.S. Cavalry horse Comanche

This former Kansan lived in a little house on the prairie around Independence. Who was she?
Laura Ingalls Wilder

Where was the first Dillon's store?
Sterling in Rice County

In 1540, Francisco Vasquez de Coronado was in search of what when he came to Kansas?
The seven cities of Cibola

The first Kansas star in the American flag was raised over the Hall of Independence in Philadelphia by whom?
Newly elected President Abraham Lincoln

In 1872, how many bison hunters were operating out of Dodge City?
2,000

Who was the first husband of the Duchess of Windsor, and where was he born?
Earl Winfield Spencer was born in Kinsley.

What was added to the Kansas flag in 1961?
The word "Kansas"

What towns bill themselves as the Catfish Capital of the World?
Chetopa and Oswego, both on the Neosho River

When the Corwin-Churchill team from Bismarck, N.D., won the first National Baseball Congress national tournament in Wichita in 1935, who was the team's pitcher?
Satchel Paige

What is the state animal?
North American bison

What was the name of the first steamer to enter the Kansas River?
The Western Engineer

How many people lived in Topeka at the time Kansas joined the Union?
300

What was the most-traded item carried on the Santa Fe Trail?
Cotton goods

When did The Kansas Weekly Herald, Kansas' first regular English weekly newspaper, first publish?
Sept. 15, 1854

In what year did German Mennonites start coming to Kansas?
1874

How many electoral votes does Kansas have?
Seven

About the author

Charlotte Harper

Steve Harper, 53, is a third-generation Kansan who lives in Newton with his wife, Charlotte, and daughters Alicia, Rachel and Audrey. The Harper home has been in the family since it was built in 1908 by Grant Merrell, Harper's great-uncle.

Harper's maternal family, the Merrells and Finnells, moved to Kansas from Ohio and Tennessee in the late 1880s. They settled west of Newton along West Emma Creek near what is now called Twin Bridges. Following World War I the bridges were dedicated to the memory of Lauren Finnell, Harper's great-uncle, and Arthur Whitesell, the first Harvey Countians to be killed in World War I.

Harper graduated from Newton High School in 1962. He served in the United States Air Force from 1963 to 1967. In 1971 he earned a bachelor's degree in motion pictures from Brooks Institute of Photography and Fine Arts in Santa Barbara, California.

In November 1971 he became the production department manager of the Audio-Visual Center at Wichita State University and in the summer of 1972 he joined the faculty of the department of graphic design at WSU's College of Fine Arts. He taught there for a year, during which time he was also an adjunct member of the fine arts graduate faculty.

From May 1974 through December 1979 he was the photojournalism instructor in the journalism department in the College of Liberal Arts at WSU, as well as teaching several courses in motion pictures for the speech department. During that time he also worked as a photo-stringer for United Press International and the Associated Press.

In 1980 he became director of photography for The Wichita Eagle-Beacon, and in July 1989 became senior photographer, working on Kansas day trip stories and other self-assigned stories. In October 1989 he became the newspaper's outdoor writer.

He has won 15 regional and national awards in photojournalism and has been active in the fine arts, participating in 11 photography exhibitions including three one-man shows. His Outdoor pages have twice been named "Best Newspaper Outdoor Page of the Year" by the Outdoor Writers Association of America. In 1995 he was named Conservation Communicator of the Year by the Kansas Wildlife Federation.

Although he left education in 1979, Harper has continued to teach photography through workshops and seminars as well as teaching two semesters of photojournalism at Kansas State University. He also conducts Kansas Day Trip Bus Tours.